T0380669

JUST IMAGINE

The Joy of God's Hospitality Overflowing
with Loving Relationships

DIANNE B. SALTER

WESTBOW
PRESS®
A DIVISION OF THOMAS NELSON
& ZONDERVAN

WestBow Press books may be ordered through booksellers or by contacting:

WestBow Press
A Division of Thomas Nelson & Zondervan
1663 Liberty Drive
Bloomington, IN 47403
www.westbowpress.com
1 (866) 928-1240

Cover Painting: Amaya Sanford

ISBN: 978-1-9736-6056-9 (sc)
ISBN: 978-1-9736-6055-2 (e)

Library of Congress Control Number: 2019904635

Print information available on the last page.

WestBow Press rev. date: 7/30/2019

To the memory of my parents,
Paul and Ruby Byers

Paul welcomed everyone; for him, no one was a stranger.
Ruby hosted all; for her, each was an honored guest.

CONTENTS

INTRODUCTION

Let's Start at the Very Beginning

God ... then radiant light, breathtaking beauty, perfect paradise: welcoming,
overflowing, fervent love *to humans created in the very image of God.*
Then, paradise lost ... but wait—not all is lost. *God's steadfast love endures forever.*
Fast-forward through the ages.
God becomes flesh and dwells among us—Jesus—an invitation to all!
Arms outstretched on the cross, expressing lavish love for every person ever created.
And on the ground, room—infinite room—at the foot of the cross for everyone.
Ultimate, forgiving love: amazingly unconditional,
Offering acceptance into the eternal family of God.

A Call to Love

The story above of a creative and prevailing love is my story of being enfolded in God's relentless, divine love. My parents lived God's love in our home and church. Such love was multiplied hundreds of times through the nurture of extended family, our church family, and other Christian relationships in my path. God's presence was with me. Step by step, his call led me. Following Jesus is a life-changing action story.

The love Jesus selflessly offers me, I am to imitate to others, so they too might experience ultimate, forgiving love. Then *they* will be urged to embrace others with that love; Jesus' love is never meant to be just received. A scene from a movie I viewed years ago at a youth gathering has etched that truth upon my mind.

In the movie, a stylish lady is making her way to an event at church. Opening the gate of the fence that protects the building, she seems more than oblivious to the onlookers from the neighborhood. Deliberately, she closes the gate and continues on, failing to acknowledge any of the neighbors. The children peer through the fence, while the adults watch and walk away. The narrator of the movie abruptly asks, "Is this the church of Jesus Christ?"

Whatever her reason, the lady did not reflect love; Jesus' love is always meant to be passed along.

That night God planted a seed in my heart and mind, a subtle but persistent desire to be a partner in his plan for the church of Jesus Christ—connecting with, welcoming, and loving others into his kingdom.

Recognizing Barriers

How does one help a culture see the grand scope of God's hospitality—the essence of the gospel? How could I help those of us already in the church to be more intentional with active, welcoming acceptance, expressing God's love for each person and inviting them into the family of God?

In visiting various churches and interviewing members, problems became evident. There were often subtle and initially unseen barriers. More visible were cavalier attitudes and behaviors unbecoming of children of God anywhere but certainly in God's house. Some churches were apathetic toward newcomers; others had isolated themselves from people who were different. To the extreme was an ambiance that suggested closing—even locking—gates, hearts.

Practices of loving outreach and invitation often seemed nonexistent. There appeared to be little or no concern for folks without faith or outside the walls of the church. Vital questions—"Isn't God's love for everyone?" and "How is that love being offered?"—were not answered well.

Further light was shed on these barriers during an interview with Eric, a student in high school. I asked if he felt his church was hospitable. He paused for a moment and then replied, "I would have to say no because I know *I'm* not hospitable." With wisdom beyond his years, he acknowledged his lack of hospitality and concluded that anyone who encountered him would not sense God's loving welcome.

Pursuing God's Purpose

To this day, I value Eric's frank admission. It represents the crux of the problem this book addresses, and hopefully will inspire solutions. I have tried to make God's vision of love and hospitality my vision; I pray you will too. The book is written in four parts, with hope that you will find spiritual growth somewhere along the spectrum of God's hospitality.

Part I: What Is God's Hospitality?
           More than coffee and doughnuts, it's about our relationships with God and others.

Part II: Why Do We Extend God's Hospitality?

It is God's plan throughout scripture that we are to learn, teach, and practice the way to love.

Part III: Who Is Called to Extend God's Hospitality?

Every Christian and every church are given responsibility for the ministry of Christ's welcoming acceptance.

Part IV: How Are We to Live Out God's Hospitality?

When we live for Christ, not ourselves, it will pull us from our comfort zones. We need to depend upon the Spirit of God to empower us.

Because you have begun reading this book, I believe God is placing in your heart and mind a desire to help enact his plan of welcoming and loving others into the kingdom—and by way of your church.

We *can* and *must* navigate barriers, discomforts, and even fears of opening our lives and churches to strangers. It often requires seemingly countless course corrections, but we know our compass is the Word of God. So as you sail this sea of discipleship, be assured the wind of the Spirit will be at your back. Sail on!

PART I

What Is God's Hospitality?

It's about Relationships

CHAPTER 1

Living a Life of Love: Helping Hearts Come Home

Imitate God ... because you are his dear children.
Live a life filled with love, following the example of Christ.
He loved us and offered himself as a sacrifice for us,
A pleasing aroma to God.
—Ephesians 5:1–2 (NLT)

Everybody's home, Ruby thought as she smiled and locked the door. She was often heard to say, "There is no better feeling than knowing all your family is home." Her life was based on the assertion that in all our goings and comings, home is where hearts connect.

Ruby worked hard to make a house a home. She was a mother hen who gathered her chicks faithfully and protectively under her wing. She tirelessly provided for their needs, exemplifying tangible love.

In Jesus' practical teaching, he tells a story pointedly relating to such love. He refers to a mother hen securing her chicks because she loves them more than her own comfort and safety—even her life.

That was Ruby, but her love and care went beyond the immediate family. A lifestyle of kindness and hospitality touched many lives. Extended family, friends, and others who needed encouragement or a place to connect were often in her home. A beloved, widowed sister and her young son were always welcome. A Jewish couple who had lost their apartment needed a place to live, so she rented the extra bedroom at a very low rate, preserving their dignity.

The Hobo Network knew Ruby's house. Homeless men would jump on and off the train as it was passing through town. When one came to her back door, she extended hospitality by offering uplifting words, good food, and a place on the porch to sit and eat. Often children—some from the Children's Home and some who were relatives needing extra TLC—joined the family on weekends and for holiday celebrations. Those who stayed the night into Sunday morning understood that everyone in the house would attend church.

Ruby's husband, Paul, was a wonderful, hardworking provider. While never very helpful with indoor chores, he furnished everything needed to make their home a place of welcome and warmth. Many times, without notice, he invited people home. Impromptu gatherings of acquaintances or business friends often occurred at the kitchen table. Ruby amiably greeted these guests and gladly prepared tasty meals.

Paul enjoyed all types of people, but he had a special place in his heart for the underdog. Some who needed a job, even if their background wasn't great, were hired to work in his small business. They were often given second and third chances to do better. Paul's invitation to "talk through some things" was not unusual. More than one benefited from his understanding and compassion.

Regardless of anyone's faith, or lack thereof, Ruby and Paul treated all graciously. Time and time again, recipients of their hospitality commented that the hosts were living their Christianity. People would even ask them about their faith, opening marvelous moments for simple faith sharing.

In church, a priority was helping people feel included and at home. Creating lovely receptions and fellowship times was Ruby's gift. Perhaps unaware that throughout scripture, food was a unifying expression of welcome, a common denominator, she believed it was a genuine way to relate to others. When food was served and shared in love, it had power to bond. Walking through the congregation and shaking hands with everyone was Paul's love; it was his way to connect. Newcomers and those who had been away for a while were given special attention. Together, Ruby and Paul prepared the elements and organized the serving of Holy Communion. This sacred task and all their work for the church afforded them many opportunities to invite, include, and help people feel at home—now in God's house.

Had you asked this couple why they so actively loved others and sacrificed much, they very likely would have said, "That's what Christians are to do."

Being in agreement, we as God's children are to live lives reflecting that conviction. We are to imitate God, including loving as God loves. Our model is Christ, who loves each one of us and gave himself for us. Like a beautiful, fragrant flower, we are to attract folks and give off the aroma of the love of Christ. People should be able to detect our scent and gently inhale God's love that transforms human behavior, perhaps even belief. This *is* our purpose!

Ruby and Paul were no more perfect than anyone else. But in their faith journeys, they tried to be true to the scriptures. The foundation of their beliefs was a Savior who loves and forgives. Their grateful response was to live lives of love by sharing their time, their possessions, and their faith.

Good News for All the People

Now, as then, our churches are made of people like Paul and Ruby—imperfect people. Thus, every church is imperfect. Yet since creation began, the drumbeat of God's love has resounded. Despite human failings, the psalmist was aware of this cadence when he sang, "God's steadfast love endures forever … God's steadfast love endures forever," measure after measure after measure (Psalm 136 CEV).

Ever since Adam and Eve fell out of step with God, creation has been broken. However, God's intent has always been that his covenant people bring the salvation story to this sin-filled world. Coming to earth in Jesus, God achieved what the entire Old Testament had been moving toward.[1] Those of us who have experienced the incredible steadfast love of God through Jesus are to live the story of Jesus and his love, sharing it with others.

What does Jesus offer? In him, all nations, all peoples, are now called to be covenant people. Jesus lived not to please himself but to show us how to be humble, obedient partners in God's saving plan. In Jesus, we have a Savior. He is a bedrock who offers love, forgiveness, hope, transformation, new life, and life eternal. In Jesus, we are the body of Christ to a broken and hurting world; we become the church, offering to others what we have accepted. As the angels said, "Good news to all people."

No one, other than the covenant people of God, takes this wonderful message of reconciliation to our communities and our world. There *is* no other plan; the church must build the kingdom of God! We seek God's presence and preparation for the labor ahead through prayer, praise, worship, and study. And although the Spirit fills us to overflowing so that we might demonstrate the goodness of God to a waiting and watching world, we must be intentional. The body of Christ reaches for, invites, and brings others to know the one true God made known to us most fully in Jesus Christ. But how, in this present age, can we best grow God's kingdom?

Hospitality in the American Culture

The task within our homes and churches is large. It necessitates that we go against the cultural norm. Over the last 150 years, the practice in our culture has been to offer hospitality to only our biological families and close friends.[2] That precedent challenges the ideal melting pot view of America. More important, it violates God's intention for the world. Unfortunately, there seems to have developed an element within the human heart that causes us to erect our defenses against the stranger.[3]

In short, America is becoming privatized. We often live in our own houses, separated from others by our own private driveways. We seldom sit on the front porch or congregate as neighbors. We seem to prefer the back of the house, often with a fence or hedge around it. Clubs and social groups tend to be private. Privacy laws abound everywhere. Some might ask, "And the problem is what?"

Some privacy is not just desirable but necessary. People feel vulnerable; they want to protect themselves within their *space*. The problem is people are hoarding privacy by avoiding much face-to-face interaction. But meaningful relationships, real hospitality, and genuine love cannot coexist with extensive isolation. We must welcome others into our space, and if invited, we must be ready to enter theirs. Oh yes, we may be vulnerable—and blessed—as was Jesus.

God calls to all, "Come and see. Come to My house and see the love I have for you." Mi casa es su casa. (My house is your house.) That is God's way of welcoming people. My family has received this kind of invitation and fantastic hospitality in parts of the Spanish-speaking world.

Language is not the issue. Language is not the barrier. But discomfort with *strangers* can initiate issues and build barriers that reinforce privatized lives. For those who know God's love and want to share it, step out in faith. Make a stranger an acquaintance and an acquaintance a friend. Speak the language of your heart, punctuated by your actions.

In North American and some European cultures, intentional welcoming is provided by the commercial world. Shopping marts have friendly greeters at doors, extending welcome to all who enter. Corporations have hospitality rooms at conventions. They furnish lavish spreads that are free to all who have been invited. A popular Italian American restaurant used to send cordial words into our homes via television. "We offer *hospitalia*. When you're here, you're family." What a wonderful thought—an invitation to belong.

We, in our churches, can learn from the commercial world. Companies use hospitality to help consumers feel appreciated and comfortable. The hope is they will buy what companies make available: goods and services. Churches can use hospitality to help others feel wanted and valued. The hope is they will partake in all that God makes available: many supportive, loving relationships with God's people; an intimate, loving relationship with our great God; and all the goodness and service that will follow.

The Scriptures Demonstrate Hospitality

Along with the Hebrew scriptures, the ancient Greek and Near East cultures communicate the tradition of receiving the stranger. The Old Testament teaches the people of Israel to welcome others as God welcomes them; a sacred bond is conceived between host and guest.

In the New Testament, the kingdom vision is a movement in which Jesus aims at nothing less than the transformation of human society.[4] The hospitality Jesus offers is a sanctuary for all to feel honored as children of God. It is a place in which to grow into the likeness of Christ Jesus.

Hospitality in God's House

Within the Christian community, our motivation and hope should be God's love for the whole world. In fact, this love was so enormous that God came to visit, and in Jesus Christ, he gave himself for all people. When we are cognizant of this triumph and realize we are children of God, it is incumbent upon us to invite others into the divine family.

By providing hospitality in God's house, we establish a household. In this household of faith, we learn to love, nurture, and help others recognize themselves as children of God. When we embrace the truth that God's steadfast love continues and we desire that all become part of the family, we contend that God's household never gets too big. Our words and actions must express and live out that everyone is welcome in God's house. The entire environment and sensibility must create a vibrant outflow that says to newcomers, reluctant attendees, and "regulars" alike, "We are so glad you are here. We want you to feel at home!"

Love Leads People Home

Now consider what occurs in our churches. We sing, teach, and preach about a God who beckons to all with love. Yet there is no meaning apart from helping others to experience that love. The most engaging music played and sung, the most profound lessons taught, and the most spirited sermons preached about God's supreme love in Christ Jesus become dissonant sounds in a setting where that love is not practiced with an intentional plan for sharing its source.

But when members assume specific responsibilities for hospitality, God's love begins to flow, and many *get it*. They are aware of *becoming* the church of Jesus Christ, aware they are the ones building the kingdom of God. And most assuredly, they understand there *is* a place for everyone!

For a church to be God's house, for us to be Christ's church, we must imitate God. The ever-present drumbeat of love that led us home still stirs our hearts. God's cadence connects. It inspires, encourages, and empowers us to help other hearts come home.

Hospitality Challenge

1. Ponder this:
    a. How does hospitality differ from entertaining?
    b. Write *your* definition of hospitality.
2. Ask yourself: When was the last time I invited someone, other than biological family or close friends, to join me anyplace?
3. Name or describe as many characteristics of God's love as you can.
4. Discuss what it means to be a child of God.
5. Contemplate and discuss each of the following:
    a. God's loving someone has absolutely nothing to do with our liking or not liking the person.
    b. What difficulties does that present for us as we strive to imitate God?

Prayer: O God, thank you for loving me! May the assurance of that love beat forever in my soul. Help me to accept that I am called to imitate the way you love. Teach me to live a life of love, as Christ loves all. Amen.

CHAPTER 2

Timeless: God, Love, Home, Welcome

Even the sparrow finds a home,
And the swallow a nest for herself,
Where she may lay her young, at your altars,
O LORD of hosts, my King and my God.
Happy are those who live in your house,
Ever singing your praise.
—Psalm 84:3–4 (NRSV)

In our family, spoken in both truth and jest, we declared some certainties in life: taxes and change. Undoubtedly change is inevitable. But scripture teaches us about steadfast and timeless facets of life. God's love is forever constant, and we depend upon it for our basic human needs. From generation to generation, basic human needs have not changed, but how they are satisfied has. Upon recognizing that someone may be hungry or homeless, you might give a couple of coupons for Big Mac meals or a quick twenty dollars. Those are acts of kindness and goodness. However, they lack the welcome of a homemade meal and the warmth of a caring conversation that people like Ruby and Paul would have provided. Their gifts made folks feel wanted, valued, and at home.

Every living creature needs a home. Thousands of years ago, the psalmist wrote, "Even the sparrow finds a home." People are at home when their hearts connect with the hearts of others. We who love God and know that God loves us are already home; our hearts are joined.

But we must respond to the needs of others, forge new links, and share tangible expressions of God's love. With the guidance and power of the Holy Spirit, we can show others love and how to love and help hearts connect. We can help others be at home with us and God, where, in unison, we rejoice and sing praises at the altar of God.

Such was the case with Mikie. As a child, he came to Paul and Ruby's house for weekend visits. Life was difficult for him, and he often acted inappropriately. His visits frequently included expletives and behavioral challenges. Still, he was loved unconditionally and was fully part of the family while in their home. Gently yet firmly, Mikie was taught right choices. As he was touched by many within their extended family, God's love flowed into his very being.

For many years, there was no contact with Mikie. Then one day, unexpectedly, a relative of mine happened upon him. In a friendly exchange, he said, "I am the man I am today because of Paul and Ruby." Mikie had felt welcomed and loved. He connected and belonged; he felt at home. By way of grace through servants of God, Mikie had been transformed.

It's important to be reminded that many in our world haven't experienced a home that encompasses such love. God's plan is that all who claim to be loved by God are to provide opportunities for others to dwell in God's love—a "place" called home.

What Is Home?

Home is a place; it is also a provision. Home is love and care that provide a deep sense of belonging that saturates the core of our inner selves, our hearts. On a cross-stitch picture I retrieved from Grandma's house were these words:

> No matter how small it is …
> No matter how large it is …
> A family together means home.

There is a story of a little fellow who understood this definition of home. New to the classroom, his teacher asked him, "Where do you live?" When he couldn't give an immediate answer, she anxiously continued, "Don't you have a home?" With eyes open wide, he quickly replied, "Oh yes, we have a home. We just don't have a house to put it in yet." This little guy belonged; he had a family. When they were together, he knew he was home.

Home is the place that when we go there, they have to take us in.

Recall the story of the prodigal son, who left home after demanding and receiving his part of the inheritance (Luke 15). He squandered it all, living on the fast track. When he came to his senses, he wanted to return home. He realized home was where his heart was. He was willing to live as one of the hired hands; he simply wanted to be home. He hoped his father and family, whom he had exploited and left behind, would accept him back. The runaway son was banking on home being the place where they would have to take him in.

Perhaps a title for this story could be "The Loving Father." The son was a great way off when the father, having unconditional love, was impelled to run to receive his lost son. Overjoyed, the father embraced him. He clothed him with garments, wrapping him in love. Referenced in the

Old Testament, these garments symbolized salvation and righteousness. He put a ring on his son's finger to claim him as family and put sandals on his feet to help him walk rightly.

This father even engaged others in the household to help throw a bountiful party in celebration of the homecoming. Feasting on the coveted fatted calf—only the best of food—fortified this bonding event. The love of this father moved beyond just taking in his son; it was about the son coming home where he belonged. This exceptional Father is God. No matter how far away anyone strays, God wants to have an intimate, loving relationship with them. God wants them home.

We, like the elder son, are the helpers God entrusts to manage the homestead; we are the faithful family members who stay close to home. In this story, God reminds us that even when people come home when we don't expect them, they are meant to be there as part of God's family. God's abundant resources and love are available for all. Though we may be reluctant, we must learn to love who God loves—everyone. God counts on us to throw a joyful party when someone—anyone—comes home to God's family. Homecomings make God smile, and we are blessed as we partner in loving them home!

In the children's storybook *The Runaway Bunny,* author Margaret Wise Brown illustrates the same love. As the mother bunny reminds her little bunny, he will never go anywhere that she will not follow him with her love. For the mother bunny, nothing is too much bother or too risky. She wants her little bunny home.

Home Is Where Our Story Begins

Created out of love by the one true God, all are united with God, making each of us of great worth. But many do not know this. We must learn to recognize God as the source of our worth and to love God in return. God's masterful design is to have instruction begin by receiving and practicing loving nurture within our natural families, our earthly homes. A healthy home is a laboratory of love where hearts become contagious with love. Then God wants us to infect people beyond our immediate family, starting an epidemic that cannot be contained.

Unfortunately, many earthly homes have not been exposed to enough love to get it. There may be ignorance or rejection of God's love. Many utterly do not realize the value God has placed upon them and all others. What people have not learned, they cannot live. What they have not been given, they cannot give.

Can their immunity to love be broken? With God's help, we must try. Love does not wait to be solicited but selflessly seeks to provide for the needs of others. Speak for God's heart; show people how precious they are. Teach them to love one another as they learn to love themselves. Help people begin a new story; help them secure a new home.

Home Is Being Enfolded in God's Love

Love is the epitome of God's character. Love is the purpose of God's creation.
God is the source of love. We are the product of love. And creation continues.
God is self-perpetuating. Love is self-perpetuating. God *is* love.
In church, God's house, any and all can dwell in the presence of God and be draped in love.
The psalmist knew of being in God's presence.

> The one thing I ask of the Lord—the thing I seek the most—
> Is to live in the house of the Lord all the days of my life,
> Delighting in the Lord's perfections and meditating in his Temple.
> For he will conceal me there when troubles come …
> Hear me when I pray, O Lord. Be merciful and answer me!
> My heart has heard you say, "Come and talk to me."
> And my heart responds, "Lord, I am coming." (Psalm 27:4–5, 7–8 NLT)

In scripture, a church is referred to as *the body of Christ*. God's love is made known to us most completely in Christ Jesus. Thus, those in a church who love and worship God, who desire to serve and represent Jesus, are charged with sharing God's full provision of love and resources with others. We glorify God when we encourage people to come into God's house, encounter the love of God, and consider making the church their new home.

Home Is Where God Hopes Our Eternal Dwelling Place Will Be

Being in the presence of God for all eternity is the ultimate meaning of home. In conversation with a woman who had just lost her husband, she spoke of incredible comfort in knowing he had gone home. It had been a lengthy goodbye. Although he no longer recognized her, he responded to her voice. During his last hours, she tenderly repeated again and again, "I love you." Assured of her love and now anticipating God's eternal love, he replied, "I want to go home." By the grace of God, he did. There is a void in God's heart that will not be filled until everybody's home!

Again, the psalmist expresses the allure and desire to be in God's house: "Happy are those who live in your house" (Psalm 84:4a NRSV). Being home is the promise and provision of our mutual indwelling with God: God in us and us in God. It can begin in this life and continue for life eternal. "Surely goodness and love will follow me all the days of my life, and I will dwell in the house of the LORD forever" (Psalm 23:6 NIV).

What Is Welcome?

Welcome has many uses.

Verb: We *welcome* others by helping each to feel at home when they are not at home, as Christ does us.

Noun: A cordial *welcome* to come be with us in church is a step toward coming and being with Jesus himself.

Adjective: And upon feeling at home with love from God and us, a most *welcome* response is to share that love with others.

Nearly every church thinks it is friendly and accepting of others, when in reality, few regularly exhibit pleasant, welcoming practices. God's house is to be a place where love is dispersed among and dispensed through the family of God within. Many churches need to take on a different aroma of welcome and love that clings to all who enter—and God wants the fragrance to last.

It is an exercise in futility to sing, teach, and preach about a God of love if our places of worship are not settings that say to all people, "Welcome. Come experience God's love." While we tend to love and care for each other in our congregations, we need to focus on those who are not part of a church family. We must continually evaluate whether outsiders feel welcome in our churches.

Cindy, Bruce, and their family were new in the community. Hoping to rebuild their lives, they realized that being in God's house with God's people was an important part of the foundation. Many attempts to find a promising church had failed. And when they drove into the parking lot of the big yellow-brick church, they were not excited. But after entering the building, their spirits began to rise. Several people greeted them with wholehearted acceptance. Cindy and Bruce felt God's presence; God had embraced them. Within a very few minutes, their eyes met and said, "This is it!" The welcome they had received helped them sense they were home.

Churches that represent the body of Christ should pull out all the stops to establish an operative ministry of inclusion. All people are to receive a warm welcome and to feel at home. This will not happen effectively and consistently without an intentional plan and trained persons in place. Whether folks come on their own initiative as visitors, are brought by someone as guests, or are members who have been absent or disconnected for some time, they are to be and feel wanted. Aware that others want them there is affirmation that *God* wants them there.

Even though personalities differ, there is to be a perception of connecting to a family. Almost everyone responds well to a friendly welcome. Even people who want to preserve their space like to feel that others are mindful of their presence. However, there are limits to how much *welcome* people appreciate. Some are overwhelmed if they are greeted with too much exuberance. A greeting is pleasant only if it puts the person at ease. Learning and applying gentle ways to approach and relate to people will help to determine their comfort level. We relate differently with each member of our own families. We must be prepared to do so with anyone who is or may become a partner in our church families.

To present God's kind of welcome, we must upgrade our hospitality quotient. As people of God, we are to "honor God by accepting each other, as Christ has accepted you" (Romans 15:7 CEV) The pinnacle is reached when we welcome each person *as if they were Christ!*

Hospitality Challenge

1. Refer to the commentary on the prodigal son. Describe the significance of the difference between these two versions:

    the father ... was impelled to run to meet his lost son.
    the father ... was impelled to run to receive his lost son.

2. Mary Engelbreit calendars, infused with her artistry and the sayings of others, have brought me simple pleasures and benchmarks for living. Here are some offerings from her Home Calendar:

- Home is where there's one to love us (Charles Swain).
- Home, the spot on earth supremely blest, a dearer, sweeter spot than all the rest. (Robert Montgomery).
- Where thou art, that is home (Emily Dickinson).
- Lord, this humble house we'd keep sweet with play and calm with sleep. Let thy *love* and let thy *grace* shine upon our dwelling place (Edgar A. Guest).
- A house is a home when it shelters the body and comforts the soul (Phillip Moffitt).
- When there is room in the heart, there is room in the house (Danish proverb).

    Which of those sayings provides benchmarks for you or your church?

3. What specific creative practices can be implemented that could help people feel at home when they aren't at home? Consider this for your church, your home, and other social settings.

4. Discuss what is meant by "Love is self-perpetuating."

5. Some years ago, there was a popular Christian slogan, "God doesn't make junk." Perhaps a more powerful proclamation would have been, "God only makes precious jewels." We look at people through human eyes. So treating everyone as if they aren't junk can be quite demanding. How difficult would it be to treat them as precious jewels? But Christians are to see people through God's eyes. And to God, each person is of great worth—a most precious jewel.

    Brainstorm ways to convince both yourself and others of this vital truth. Share your thoughts.

Prayer: Gracious God, thank you for creating me with a longing to come home. Thank you for your welcome and wanting me to dwell with you. It is so very good to be in your presence, to feel your love. Create in me now a deep desire to help *others* know how much you love them. I want to join them in savoring your love. I want to partner with you in welcoming them home. Amen.

CHAPTER 3

God's Royal Decree: We Are to Extend God's Hospitality

Jesus told this story: "The gatekeeper opens the gate for him (the shepherd), and the sheep hear his voice. He calls his own sheep by name and leads them out … I am the gate for the sheep … Whoever enters by me will be saved … I came that they may have life, and have it abundantly … I am the good shepherd. I know my own and my own know me, just as the Father knows me and I know the Father. And I lay down my life for the sheep. I have other sheep that do not belong to this fold. I must bring them also, and they will listen to my voice. So there will be one flock, one shepherd … My sheep hear my voice. I know them, and they follow me."

—John 10:3, 7, 9–10, 14–16, 27 (NRSV)

"I am home where I belong. I know I am a loved and forgiven child of God. It feels so right." God yearns for every person to know they belong, to feel at home. For those who do, God wants them to gratefully and lovingly welcome others home. But God is often disappointed. A second-career pastor, who had been a bartender prior to entering a life with Christ, told his congregation, "There is more welcome for people at the brass bar than at most churches."

Perhaps you remember the TV series *Cheers*, in which imbibing and conversing comprised the pastime. The theme song was "where everybody knows your name, and they're always glad you came." It would be wonderful if that were true about our churches. Every individual is created with a deep longing to be known, valued, connected, and loved. Every individual is created to be home—with God.

Our church families are to help those outside the church find their way home. We should know them for who they are; value them for whose they are; and together, love them by showing

15

them Jesus. We, as the body of Christ, can do a much better job than we are doing. But we need inspiration, guidance, and courage. What does Jesus offer? Cheryl Somers-Ingersol reminds us:

> Jesus does know us—the good and the bad, the gracious and the petty, the lovely and the ugly, the hopes and the fears, the achievements and the failures—the whole truth of our being. He knows us completely and still promises us a relationship with him (and thereby with the Father) that is imperishable. Jesus assures us that when we believe (give our hearts to him), we will recognize his voice so we can follow. And as we believe and hear and follow, we enter into life in his name. [1]

Jesus' own words tell us that "freely you have received; freely give" (Matthew 10:8b NIV). Jesus challenges us, the church, to help others know and love him because he knows and loves them. Jesus calls each congregation, each household of God, to continually share and live our faith with those not yet home. However, achieving this can be disputable. Inviting and welcoming the stranger, who may have additional needs, can put a burden on the household. Members might find people with certain appearances, mannerisms, or lifestyles to be distasteful or disruptive, testing the very fabric of the family. The question is whether being open and loving to all is God's will. What should be the standard of welcome for their church?

Jesus made loving others clear. He taught this truth to his original disciples, and it became an issue among them. In this mixture of men were interpersonal tensions. Having different backgrounds, opinions, and demeanors, it took a major effort by these strangers to welcome one another. The disciples became the research group of kingdom hospitality. Jesus made every effort to prevent his followers from closing the door on their neighbors. [2] Still today, he nudges all who follow him that God's heart yearns for everyone. Hospitality too is timeless.

God's Hospitality

An intentional plan for being God's ambassadors is to welcome and love others home.

Hearing of hospitality elicits thoughts and expectations of comfort, connection, and refreshment. As Christians, we become hosts who offer the love of Christ, a love that will not disappoint. Our hospitality challenge, in all occasions, is to make people feel worthy and loved by God and us. We step into the challenge by helping them feel at home in God's house. We continue to stride forward by introducing or reinforcing the kind of relationship God desires with them. Led by the Spirit to extend hospitality in our respective churches, we become forerunners for the hospitality God makes available to all.

The word *hospitality* is rooted in the Latin word *hospes*, meaning host, guest, or stranger. *Hostis*, closely related, means stranger or enemy (one who is hostile). In one sense, there is a fine line between *host* and *hostile;* in another, they are worlds apart. The breadth of the chasm depends upon how the stranger is perceived and treated. Being hosts, we are expected to provide hospitality; being hostile, we are not. In fact, being anything less than hospitable is often viewed as being hostile. With that interpretation, we can choose to offer hospitality, or, by default, *we have chosen* to offer hostility.

Hate presents a hostile environment, as does indifference. To be ignored as a person can be more painful than to be treated as an enemy. Christians are always summoned to imitate our gracious Host by welcoming others into God's kingdom of love. Just like hate, indifference toward anyone is not condoned by God.

Hospes is also the root word for *hospital.* We know a hospital as a place of helping and healing. A neighbor once said, "The church is to be a hospital for sinners, not a museum for saints." Yes, in truth, all who are part of God's family through Christ are called saints.[3] They are simply people accepted by God as perfect, by means of the cross and not by their own doing. Yet we saints, who claim Christ as our Lord, often treat each other and strangers in a hurtful, unsaintly manner. We retain our bent to sin.

If our churches became hospitals for sinners, we could live the teachings of Jesus in life-giving ways: we could help, heal, and give hope to each other and those yet to be connected with us. As believers, our expectation is that God or Christ or the Holy Spirit will play a role in every hospitable transaction.[4]

In rendering hospitality with the intent to connect with others, Henri Nouwen says, "It is the Christ in you, who recognizes the Christ in me."[5] Lovett Weems, teaching in a seminar, put forth a practical way to reach for others. He charges us to relate to everyone with a "presumption of Grace."[6] In other words, as people of God, we must remember that the kingdom of God is the kingdom of right relationships. God's grace, available to all, embodies the fruit of the Spirit that equips us to mold right relationships. To live this out, John Henry, Cardinal Newman exhorts us to be people *radiating Christ* everywhere we go.[7] Our churches, without exception, should emit such radiance.

God's hospitality comprises these intentions:

- helping people feel welcome in God's house
- realizing that the responsibility for hospitality is on the Christian host
- welcoming strangers and offering friendship, even if they are different from us
- inviting and bringing people into an environment that will encourage and enable personal relationships with God
- living in our homes, neighborhoods, jobs, and churches in ways that radiate and imitate Christ Jesus
- implementing Hebrew hospitality, loving our neighbor, and following the apostle Paul's directives to the churches and individuals

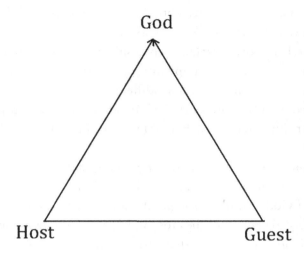

When we provide God's hospitality, something compelling often happens: such grace-filled hospitality has the wonderful potential to turn the relationship begun between host and guest into a supernatural connection that draws them together toward God.

Our God is so very hospitable—the supreme Host—whose love goes to great lengths to bring every person home as part of the household of faith. We, within the family of faith, have responded to God's pursing love. God's grand decree is that we lovingly pursue others to become our brothers and sisters in God's divine family. Each church, God's house, is to be a place that proclaims and fulfills, "Welcome home; come be part of the family."

God's Hospitality in God's House: In Search of Humility

God directs us to create an atmosphere in our churches that says to all who enter, "God wants you here." This endeavor requires that we take seriously the belief in one Lord and Father of us all. We must dispel any remnant of we/they mentality that lurks or lingers anywhere within our ministry. E. Stanley Jones says any such notion is "self-righteous pride, denoting a sense of being superior." Peter had that flaw when he said, "Though they all fall away ... I will never fall away."[8] This exposes an attitude not unlike the man who prayed, "I thank You, God, that I am not a sinner like everyone else. For I don't cheat, I don't sin, and I don't commit adultery. I'm certainly not like the tax collector!" (Luke 18:11 NLT).

As we attempt to follow God's way, having been obedient in many areas of our lives, it is so easy to fall into the trap of *pointing* when others have slipped. If we focus on the sins of others, we often fail to recognize the areas where we still fall short. It is this very issue that incites critics of the church to say we are hypocrites. A congregation fully receptive to hospitality after God's heart blurs the we/they distinction by accepting all it serves as equals with its members.[9]

Hospitality in a Complex Contemporary Culture

In a church that was seeking to be very intentional about presenting God's hospitality, people in a team were discussing the issues that prevented greater success in their particular setting. After some time, the wise pastor said, "It appears that class, cash, and clothes are the real stumbling blocks."

Our privatized culture has become ingrown and cliquish. Reaching out to connect with others is just not the modern scene. A huge complication confronting American churches is the disparity between the upper class, the middle class, and the poor. Many churches are largely white middle class. If we have had little contact with poor people, we may not understand them or their way of life. Frequently, we don't even acknowledge them. When we do, our various responses often include tasteless laughter, deliberate ignorance, numb indifference, or unfounded fear. No wonder these folks are not eager to attend our churches. So where's the love?

The other extreme of the class issue is that rich people intimidate us. We may hesitate to reach out to them because we feel they look down on us, or we are jealous of them. We might even be judgmental about what the rich have accumulated. Our pride, envy, and condemnation must be turned over to Jesus. We must believe that people with abundant wealth need the good news of God's grace, favor, and unconditional love as much as the poor, the middle class, anyone—there's the love!

People are part of diverse cultures and social classes. They have distinctive morals and belief systems. Each person is unique. The effort required to love and serve this complex of people can dampen our desire and effectiveness to deliver God's hospitality. But the strongest deterrent may very well be fear.

Fear vs. Faith: A Battle for God's Hospitality

Horror and tragedy have touched churches along with the greater society in many countries. For a long time, much of our planet knew terrorism and brutality in ways the United States did not. Since September 11, 2001, however, American life has changed. Shootings, bombings, and other forms of inhumanity have become more prevalent throughout parts of the world, and the United States has not been spared. The level of fear has increased substantially. Congregations are caught in a dilemma: how to welcome and include outsiders to our churches in a society in which violence can erupt anytime, anyplace.

Dan Dick informs and encourages to help our faith keep fear in check:

> Churches since the first century have been public gathering places and throughout history have been the location of acts of violence. Wherever human beings interact, bad (even destructive) behavior is inevitable … It is imperative that the Christian community apply the very best critical thinking skills to this issue so that faith prevails over fear.[10]

As we are diligent in our safety planning, we must remember there is always vulnerability when we welcome others to receive our love—God's love. So for God's sake, we choose to welcome, knowing we are enfolded and empowered by God.

There is always danger of fear driving decision-making in our lives, society, and congregations. Churches where members feel anxious about the neighborhood or community around them are likely to put their emphasis on security systems rather than positive outreach.[11] In a church for which this seemed to be happening, one member asked, "Are we locking Jesus in or locking him out?"

That question is pertinent and problematic, requiring a response. It is imperative for faithful Christians to allow the biblical assurance of God's leading and presence with us to outweigh the fear implanted by the sensationalism of news media. Do we hear God's voice as clearly and as often as we hear the news reports? Jesus must be present in our solution.

As we carefully and prayerfully seek answers to these questions, we should not throw caution to the wind. We must be faithful *and* vigilant. For the Christian church, it is right and good that we throw fearful tensions and dilemmas to the "wind" of the Holy Spirit, who will help us establish and implement reasonable safeguards. Evidence that the Holy Spirit is pushing us will be witnessed when we *pray together* and are moved to an answer. Facing uncertainty and trepidation, the first Christian church, driven by the Spirit's power, as recorded in Acts 2, was brought together "with one accord."

Here are some plausible safeguards:

> ➢ Install good lighting outside and inside.
> ➢ All outside doors not intended to be used as a public entrance should be locked and have a sign clearly directing where to enter the church.
> ➢ Have convenient limited entrances ministered by trained greeters and ushers.
> ➢ Doorbells should be user-friendly and have welcoming tones.
> ➢ Once inside, easy-to-follow direction signs must be in plain sight.
> ➢ Persons who connect with others are in pairs, forming a spiritual and security buddy system.
> ➢ Have persons to monitor children and youth.

> ➤ Provide accessible first aid.
> ➤ Have effective exit plans.

Whatever precautions are put in place, they must be tempered by a spirit of hospitality. The safeguards should enhance, not diminish, a sanctuary awash by grace. We should treat everyone as a welcome guest, not an unwanted intruder. We must *choose* to relate to others with a bounty of love, not the baggage of fear.

Interestingly, the word that describes the sacred place for the altar of God is *sanctuary*.

This concept emerged from the ancient Hebrew worship practices; a most sacred place, the "holy of holies", existed in the Tabernacle where only the High Priest could enter. From the Latin tradition, early Christians understood *sanctus* to mean "holy." Sanctuary, according to *Webster's*, is also a place of refuge and protection. Some churches have safe-sanctuary policies to maintain security, especially for children and teens. Christians know God to be a "place" in whom we enjoy refuge and protection. God is *our* sanctuary. We acknowledge that God is exalted, and God's house is honored by all these descriptions for sanctuary. Yet another of great importance is to be added. Christians sing of being formed into a sanctuary, as individuals and as churches: "Lord prepare me to be a sanctuary, pure and holy, tried and true. With thanksgiving, I'll be a living sanctuary to you."[12]

All people have been created for the holiness of God to dwell within them. The more pure and holy (sanctified) people become, the more of God's fullness will live in them, and the more of a sanctuary to God they will be. God prepares the people of God for *sanctification* through worship and learning in God's house, personal Bible study, actively loving, and living our faith (not fear) in the world.

Both the Old and New Testaments record God's house as "a house of prayer for all people" (Isaiah 56:7; Matthew 21:13; Mark 11:17; Luke 19:46). But this world reminds us there are many who have not yet experienced God or God's house as sanctuaries. We can view these folks as failing to measure up to our standards or as not being sufficiently holy and then fearfully think they might tarnish our church. Or we can become their spiritual refuge and protection, one by one and as a congregation. We can faithfully be their sanctuary and usher them into the sanctuary of God—shepherd them toward home.

Love: An Ally of Faith

"Do not fear" is found often throughout the Bible. John, the beloved disciple, captured the supremacy of love when he wrote, "There is no fear in love, but perfect love casts out fear" (1 John 4:18 NRSV). There are many stories in scripture by which love for God, faith in God, and being loved by God conquered fear. Here are just a few: David and Goliath, Daniel in the lions' den, the disciples in the boat amid a storm, and, most certainly, Jesus going to the cross.

> God loved the people of this world so much that he gave his only Son, so that everyone who has faith in him will have eternal life, and never really die. (John 3:16 CEV)

God commissions us to be emissaries of love. Our faith journeys will encompass fearful images, difficult obstacles, and dubious outcomes. But being connected to and dependent upon God will win the day. We need to believe this for ourselves; then God wants us to love others into that same belief.

Handwritten in the margin of my grandma's Bible, next to the twenty-third psalm, were these words: "Security is not the absence of danger; it is the presence of Jesus." He promises to be with us through it all. Jesus even goes through locked doors, those in our churches and those in our minds and hearts. He calls us to join him in the crucial campaign of expanding the kingdom of God.

The campaign hinges on winning the battle for God's hospitality. And assuredly, God wants us in the fight. We know that when love and faith are brought to bear, fear will be defeated. God wants us and our churches to faithfully welcome and love others home, where they will know peace and joy in the presence of Jesus. God *will* be victorious! Will we obey our Commander and contribute to the victory?

Contemplate this magnificent portrait of God's hospitality.

> God … Your beauty and love chase after me every day of my life.
> I'm back home in the house of God for the rest of my life. (Psalm 23:1a, 6 MSG)

We who dwell in God's presence are to invite others to receive God's love. It's a love that welcomes and chases after them—wanting them *home*!

Will L. Thompson, the hymn writer, penned it well:

> Softly and tenderly Jesus is calling, calling for you and for me;
> See, on the portals he's waiting and watching, watching for you and for me.
> Come home, come home; you who are weary, come home;
> Earnestly, tenderly, Jesus is calling, calling, O sinner, come home![13]

Hospitality Challenge

1. Look for and act upon opportunities to be the message of Jesus, helping someone not connected with any church family to come home.

2. As partners of God, in what specific ways can we learn to "know people for *who* they are and value them for *whose* they are"?

3. Discuss the meaningful difference between these prompts:
   "Enter into life in Jesus' name."
   "Enter into life in *your* name."

4. List three of your qualities that help to identify you as "a living sanctuary to God." If appropriate, compile a super-list of *different* qualities from within your group.

Prayer: Lord, help us echo *your* ways of hospitality. May I, as an individual, and we, as a congregation, never do anything that hinders people from coming into your Kingdom. May we always want to love others as you love them. Please show us how to love them well. Amen.

PART II

Why Do We Extend God's Hospitality?

It's God's Plan for Us

CHAPTER 4

Learning and Teaching the Heart of God: From Generation to Generation

For the Lord is good, his unfailing love continues forever.
And his faithfulness continues to each generation.
—Psalm 100:5 (NLT)

God's heart has always sought to bond in a loving and intimate relationship with every created person, to covenant with each one. This bond was broken when Adam and Eve disobeyed, indicating their dissatisfaction with allowing God to be God. But the Creator had no intention of letting sin be the last word.

Some have described the Bible as God's love letter to us, making God's love known. Reflect upon the nature of God's heart, as God reminded Moses of its many qualities: "God, God, a God of mercy and grace, endlessly patient—so much love, so deeply true—loyal in love for a thousand generations, forgiving iniquity, rebellion, and sin" (Exodus 34:6–7a MSG).

From the time of Abraham, God blessed the people of Israel with great gifts: a homeland, a family, and God's very presence, just because God chose to love Israel. The people were called to *bring the world back to Yahweh*, the Creator. God yearned to love and bless the entire world.

A GPS: God's Primary Sanctions

Additionally, God blessed Israel with the Torah, God's holy law. The law of the Lord was perfect. It gave the people wisdom, cohesion, strength, and direction. It would help them avoid their tendency toward fault and willful sin.

The centerpiece of the law is the Ten Commandments, designed to have the people, God's people, live as the family of God. These commands laid out a covenant agreement between the Israelites and God. The first three govern the way humans relate to God. The next two suggest how humans take care of themselves and their family. The final five cover the fundamental rules for living with other people.[1] This could rightly be called the Law of Love, meant to keep the people living in a loving, *ultimate community* with God and others—a timeless plan.

Sharing the Heart of God—Now as Then and Beyond

Expecting her first child, an excited middle-school teacher shared her joy with her students; they too were delighted about the forthcoming birth. But one day, joy was suddenly replaced by anguish; the baby's heart had stopped beating. This child would not be born alive. After four weeks of recovering from medical procedures, the teacher returned to the classroom, not knowing how to face the kids.

When she walked into her empty classroom and turned on the lights, glued to the wall were a hundred colored paper butterflies, each with a handwritten message on it from past and current students. Every message was encouraging: "Keep moving forward. Don't give up on God. And know that we love you."[2]

Interestingly, the young people in this story gave their teacher promising and prophetic words reminiscent of the provisions handed down from God in the covenant with Israel: "Press on, obey God. Stay dependent upon God. Remember, God loves you." These provisions were proclaimed by prophets of the Old Testament—over and over, generation after generation. The teacher's students had learned from some elders a way to care for and love another. These children became better prepared to teach others, including those younger, how to do the same.

A church in our community erected a beautiful addition to their facility. Engraved on a long stone, which is prominently placed, is this hope: … *so the next generation might know* (Psalm 78:6a MSG). Scripture is filled with accounts of the Lord's power—his mighty wonders and glorious deeds. Jesus insistently gave the honor to God, for Jesus acted according to the will of his Father. Thus, to know the heart of Jesus is to know the heart of Yahweh. Passing down knowledge of God from person to person, from one generation to the next, was and always will be relevant and imperative to God's plan. It is so *every person might know* and set their hope anew upon Jesus—just as God intended, just as God intends.

In the Image of God with Free Choice

Scripture says all humans have been created in the image of God. That means we have the capacity to love and serve God, to love and serve others. We can even approach becoming as holy as

God by striving to think, speak, and act as God does. We had no input into how we were created, but God has given each of us the freedom to make vitally important choices: "Do I want to live in the image of my heavenly Father? Do I want to follow the ways of God's love? Do I want to reach for the holiness of God? Well, do I?"

Why did God give us free choice? In God's wisdom, love must be a choice. We cannot truly love without choosing to love; otherwise, it would be spiritually empty manipulation. Our Creator's heart wants us to make a conscious decision to love God and love our neighbor. Jesus said there are two greatest commandments: Love God with everything you have, and love others as you love yourself.

Given the freedom to choose, we can choose wrongly. Since the moment Adam and Eve ate from the tree of knowledge of good and evil, we have been enticed to consider how very smart we are. Knowledge does help us to comprehend and conquer much in life. But just applying reason and relying solely on our own choices can lead to a defiled understanding of life. Thinking *It's my life, so I'll do whatever I feel* is seductively close to believing we don't need God or God's love. We can fail to recognize our Creator.

We smile at the story when such was true of the atheist, who was proud of his intellect. Unknowingly speaking to God, he said, "Science has progressed greatly. Surely you know we are about to make humans."

God replied, "From dust you came, and to dust you shall return."

"From dust it shall come" was the atheist's retort. With that, he bent down to scoop up some dirt.

God smiled and said, "No, no. Get your own dirt; I created that dirt."

Knowledge takes us only so far. Blaise Pascal, a seventeenth-century French mathematician, scientist, philosopher, and Christian, gave us these incredible pearls:

"The knowledge of God is far from the love of Him … It is the heart which experiences God, and not reason. This then, is faith: God felt by the heart, not by reason."[3]

By faith, we each believe the love of God is planted in our hearts for all eternity. And God was, is, and ever more shall be the very source of it all. But we each need to determine in our hearts and minds that we want to live by such faith. Then we must allow that love to fill us and manifest itself as love for God and love for others. Our supply is unbounded; the outpouring is a choice. But God does elevate the mark, wanting us to pour much love into the lives of many.

God's Love Qualities

The Exodus verses cited earlier express God's loving ways. Various biblical translations allow us to ponder their significance in a broader context. The New Revised Standard Version states God's qualities this way:

> The LORD, the LORD, a God *merciful* and *gracious, slow to anger,* and *abounding in steadfast love* and *faithfulness, keeping steadfast love* for the thousandth generation, *forgiving* iniquity and transgression and sin. (Exodus 34:6–7a NRSV; emphasis added)

Seven of God's many love qualities are described below. Scholars have contributed a workable understanding of each one. The *New Interpreter's Bible*[4] and *Nelson's Illustrated Bible Dictionary*[5] were used to compile the descriptions. Contemplate these qualities carefully. Could they be some of God's footprints for us to follow?

Merciful: This has Hebrew roots in the word *womb*, declaring that God's merciful heart yields womb-like love. A mother carrying a child in her womb nourishes and protects it with her very life. From the essence of God, love flows mercifully into our being. No matter our choices or circumstances, God's mercy is available to be accepted.

Gracious: This denotes undeserved, unmerited, without a cause kind of love. It is so amazing, so divine, that we give such love a special name—*grace*—from a gracious God. Humans receive this unearned gift through repentance and faith. It can be sought in prayer.

Slow to Anger: God never reacts in a knee-jerk fashion. God "cools off" before responding to an offense. God allows the consequences of our choices to affect us, but God is very slow to punish. Discipline, used to mold and shape, supersedes punishment. When God does get angry, it is an expression of holy love.

Abounding in Steadfast Love: God's heart is to make and keep covenant with people through intimate personal relationships. God's love is established in eternal commitment to all who will receive it.

Faithful: God is loyal, reliable, dependable, and trustworthy, desiring to be present with us, provide for us, nourish us, and restore us in all seasons of our lives.

Keeping Steadfast Love: For generation after generation, God's love has *endured*. God's love will extend beyond every tomorrow, keep on after forever, and be without end.

Forgiving: God *lifts* our violations from us, never to hold them over us again. In a broken world, a life must be taken as a substitute for sin. And the sinner must come to God's sacrifice in a spirit of repentance and faith. Jesus, our sacrificial lamb, gave his life and prayed as he died, "Father, forgive them; for they know not what they do" (Luke 23:34 KJV). Forgiveness happens as soon as we acknowledge our need for forgiveness and accept by belief the ultimate gift of love. From this divine love, we are created in the very image of God. We are God's children; we are God's heirs of salvation.

An Heirloom of Love

In the book of Deuteronomy, the people are reminded of all that God had done. God was relentless in freeing them from bondage, diligent in establishing the covenant relationship, and resolute in pursuing them to maintain their part of the covenant.

> Know therefore that the LORD your God is God; he is the faithful God, keeping his covenant of love to a thousand generations of those who love him and keep his commandments. (Deuteronomy 7:9 NIV)

The author of Deuteronomy called for the people to rededicate their lives to God. And what they had learned about God, love, and the law was to be observed and taught to their children, passed down to the next generation.

> Hear, O Israel: The LORD our God, the LORD is one. *Love the LORD your God with all your heart and with all your soul and with all your strength.* These commandments that I give you today are to be upon your hearts. Impress them on your children. Talk about them when you sit at home and when you walk along the road, when you lie down and when you get up. Tie them as symbols on your hands and bind them on your foreheads. Write them on the doorframes of your houses and on your gates. (Deuteronomy 6:4–9 NIV; emphasis added)

> And if we are careful to obey all this law before the LORD our God, as he has commanded us; that will be our righteousness. (Deuteronomy 6:25 NIV)

Those who are obedient to God, faithfully loving God, will receive a right to an inheritance.

> For you are a people holy to the LORD your God. The LORD your God has chosen you out of all the peoples on the face of the earth to be his people, *his treasured possession.* (Deuteronomy 7:6 NIV; emphasis added)

God reminded all Israel to live as one people, one family, God's family. Should any parents fail to pass on knowledge of the heart of God to their children, others were expected to fill the gap. The prophet Isaiah reassured the entire Hebrew nation of God's love and presence in their lives. The God who calls Israel by name calls *us* by name. Read Isaiah's proclamation below, substituting your name for *Jacob* and your church's name for *Israel*.

But now, GOD's Message, the God who made you in the first place, *Jacob* [insert your name], the One who got you started, *Israel* [insert your church's name]: "Don't be afraid, I've redeemed you. I've called your name. You're mine. When you're in over your head, I'll be there with you. When you're in rough waters, you will not go down. When you're between a rock and a hard place, it won't be a dead end— Because I am GOD, your personal God, The Holy of *Israel* [my italics], your Savior. I paid a huge price for you: … *That's* how much you mean to me! *That's* how much I love you! … So don't be afraid: I'm with you. (Isaiah 43:1–5a MSG)

Isaiah's proclamation affirms who God is. We can discern that "his treasured possession" is most precious indeed, and the heirloom of love is supremely secure. Isaiah continues with God's declaration of witnesses:

"But *you* are my witnesses." GOD's Decree. "You're my handpicked servant. So that you'll come to know and trust me, understand both *that* I am and *who* I am … And you know it, you're my witnesses, you're the evidence." GOD's Decree. (Isaiah 43:10, 13 MSG)

As children of God, all people are designed to live in the likeness of God, to love as God loves. Some do not know this because they do not know their Father. The Hebrews, being in covenant with God and having been declared witnesses for God, were called to invite and welcome others to come experience God's love. God's chosen people were to extend loving hospitality to everyone: friend or foe, family or stranger. God's intention was and is that all receive the inheritance of life. So we who believe in Jesus and know our Father are a covenant and chosen people of witness as well—God's decree.

Jesus Personifies Hospitality

Jesus grew up in an obedient Jewish family. A celebrated tradition in many Hebrew homes was to welcome the stranger. The hospitality that ensued was an act of obedience for "Love thy neighbor." Sensitivity to the needs of the aliens and strangers was part of Israel's experience and teaching. Families opened their homes to traveling teachers and hosted Sabbath eve supper, opening their family to others, especially those thought to be needy.[6] The scripture story of the woman who bathed Jesus' feet with her tears, dried them with her hair, and anointed them with oil is thought to be an example of one in attendance at such an evening meal.[7] Beyond the home, in this tradition some synagogues were equipped with guest rooms to accommodate overnight visitors.[8] On occasion, a stable would have to do.

God, as Jesus, came to visit. We may have thought we were *his* hosts, but he came to invite us to his heavenly home, to share the joy of an eternal feast of love—that's hospitality! Jesus modeled hospitality. As host or guest, he would humbly accept the last seat. When Jesus was a guest, he often became host to those who otherwise would have been neglected. Without an earthly home, Jesus liberally extended hospitality, frequently including food—a picnic for five thousand, a rented upper room for an intimate last meal with his disciples, a cooked breakfast on the beach for his distraught friends after his Crucifixion and resurrection.

Jesus offered rest to the heavy-laden and sanctuary to those distressed. He became angry when people were excluded. This was made evident when those not having money to purchase the proper sacrifice were being ripped off at the temple gate. Jesus exclaimed, "This is a house of prayer *for all people*; but you have made it a den of robbers" (Matthew 21:13 NKJV; emphasis added). All four gospels record this event.[9]

The life and teaching of Jesus assert that hospitality is a prime introduction to learning the heart of God and living as a child of God. Jesus completely embodies the kingdom of God. All of his words and deeds illuminate the kingdom—God's reign in the world—that is already upon us. His parables show us the love in God's heart and teach us how to live in the here and now. Jesus reaches out and invites everyone to be in the fellowship of faith, a home of believers, and the family of God. We are to follow his lead. Jesus calls us to proclaim the good news to all who will listen, being keenly watchful for folks who have never heard. We are called to teach the heart of God, increase the community of believers, and build up the kingdom of God.

Learning and teaching of the kingdom are essential in the church today. Experiences of God—living, loving, and reigning—are to be found within the hurt and brokenness of individuals, families, and congregations. We must be open to and create opportunities for sharing the wonderful, steadfast love of God—the kind of love Jesus wants to be operative in our lives and in our churches. Having a willingness to give up self is foremost. A line from a song I learned years ago floats through my mind and heart: "Love is surrender; love is surrender to his will."[10]

The Cost of Loving

Surrender was the key that unlocked God's love for the Israelites, and it remains the key for us today. Surrender requires making the choice to do what God asks, to follow how Jesus lived. Humility is a small down payment on discipleship. Selflessness is a daily price paid to provide the love of God to others. Jesus lived a life of "other-ness" and self-sacrifice. He walked his talk. In every aspect, Jesus emptied himself, totally submitting to God's will. Jesus attained the purpose poignantly described by Matthew Fox:

The lengths to which God will go to heal us are fully revealed on the cross. A costly divine forgiveness lies at the heart of the New Creation hospitality. Jesus' arms stretched on a beam extended to release our sin, to receive all in love, to invite us to new life—is the very image of God's unaccountably gracious hospitality to us.[11]

To a world that is rebellious and stiff-necked, in need of atonement for sin, what is God's response? *Yet more love!* As those who have received that priceless love at Christ's expense, we are called to surrender to a life that sacrifices self for the sake of others.

I am reminded of a prescription I heard offered to parents of children who have special needs. The physician said, "Love is the only response to help children with special needs." One parent asked, "What happens when it doesn't work?" The reply was, "Increase the dosage."

Our grandson Jacob has special needs. He has also gone through treatment for a life-threatening disease. I have watched Jacob's parents live a life of absolute self-sacrifice. I have heard our son say, "When I need to hold my son down so they can infuse cancer-killing drugs that will also kill good cells in his body, I am overcome with what God did for us." Humanity is diseased; all of us have special needs. So God increases the dosage of love for our salvation. God wants those who have been healed by love to help heal others. Be mindful of Paul's words:

> And all of this is a gift from God, who brought *us* back to himself through Christ. And God has given us this task of reconciling people to him. For God was in Christ, reconciling the world to himself, no longer counting people's sins against them. And he gave *us* this wonderful message of reconciliation. So *we* are Christ's ambassadors. God is making his appeal through *us*. *We* speak for Christ when *we* plead, "Come back to God!" (2 Corinthians 5:18–20 NLT; emphasis added)

Ambassadors for Christ

Ambassadors are those who heed the call to extend grace-filled hospitality because of the awesome hospitality God has afforded them. They are followers who look at the world and see people as God sees people—precious, beloved creations. Ambassadors commit to what God directs them to do. They are to pursue relationships with the purpose and hope that others also might be united with God. Christ has not just anointed one of us to be his ambassador but many. Christ wants his whole church to be so anointed. Together, we are assigned the ministry of reconciliation.

We, the church, are entwined in a marred and crumbling world. Many folks have fallen on hard times, and many more have only ever lived in abject poverty. Children are having children, siblings are killing each other, and often parents and adults, in general, have been pathetic role models.

Across the globe, hatred and heinous evil are becoming typical. Poverty of body, soul, and spirit is rampant. Tragically, this has been a repeated history throughout the generations.

But in every generation, churches are to mirror the heart of God in the midst of such a terrific mess. Each church is God's house, a dwelling place to be clearly marked that all are welcome. Here, God's name is holy. At home is a God of great provision—one who answers, loves, forgives, and offers a new beginning. We herald the dwelling place for what it is: a place of God's gracious hospitality to be made ready for all. We would do well to agree with what Parker Palmer says:

> The church lives under a relentless divine calling to engage in the work of reconciliation—to God, to one another and to ourselves. There is nothing about which God is more persistent than the promise that the brokenness within us and between us can and will be healed. Healing comes as a result of God's mercy and grace, not our work. But mercy and grace are channeled as the church finds ways of more fully becoming the body of Christ, whose touch heals.[12]

Scripture holds a high standard for the body of Christ to love and care for each other and to enter the company of strangers. How we welcome newcomers and strangers to our churches, withholding love from no one, is a measure of how well we know God and how ready we are to introduce God to others. The following true story is an astonishing example of such an introduction.

In 1993, Dr. Francis Collins, a physician, was asked to lead the Human Genome Project mapping DNA in humans. From his youth, Francis recalls "a heady upbringing with a downside of arrogance." His parents, who were educated at Yale, home-schooled their four sons and exposed them to many types of marvelous cultural events. Francis was sent to an Episcopal church so that he could sing in the choir. But his parents told him, "Pay no attention to what you hear from the pulpit." They were not hostile, just uninterested. So Francis became convinced that "if one believed in science, one could dispense with the need to believe in God."

Years later as a student doctor, he met Jessie at a university hospital. She suffered from a terminal illness. His job was to manage her pain. Dr. Collins was impressed by how well she accepted her condition and pain. He took notice of the wonderful stories she told about her life and family. Jessie's expressions of love, encouragement, and continual gratitude for him affected Dr. Collins deeply.

One day when he was called to her room, Jessie was clutching her chest and crying out, "Dear Jesus, take me, or take this pain away." Dr. Collins gave her the maximum dosage of medicine and remained at her bedside. Finally, the pain subsided. She loosened her grip and looked up to see her beloved physician.

Dr. Collins describes the next memorable moments:

> "Oh, Dr. Collins, you're still there. Praise the Lord." She was silent for a time …
> Then, "Dr. Collins, I have a question for you. You've stood by my bedside quite a

few days now, and I know you've heard me calling on the Lord. But you never say anything. You see how much I depend on Jesus. What do you believe?"

To my embarrassment, I felt blood rush to my face. It was the last question I expected a patient to ask … I found no answer to her question. More disturbingly, I found no explanation why suddenly I so intensely wanted an answer.

Jessie didn't survive her heart disease. But her question made me rethink everything … Just because my scientific training hadn't taught me about God, it didn't mean he wasn't here. It merely meant I hadn't considered the evidence … The deeper I looked, the more I found him … and ultimately in the person of Jesus Christ. At the age of 28, I became a believer.

On a warm summer day in 2000, President Bill Clinton announced to the world that our team had decoded and made freely available to the public "the language in which God created life." That day the President summed up for me the beautiful, durable truth that God had begun teaching me at Jessie's bedside … God is not afraid of scientific truth. How could he be? He invented it. [13]

Like the younger Francis Collins, there are many who are blind to God. When believers like Jessie relate to them and reflect the love of God upon them, they may begin to see. The world needs a great host of Jessies dispersed throughout, connected with a multitude of churches who embrace being the body of Christ. Individually and collectively, we must help others to recognize their Creator and to live in the love and manner of Christ.

Francis Schaeffer, a theologian, maintained that one generation of non-practicing Christians leads to the next generation of atheists. He states, "Oh that more of us would give our lives to train others in the Christian way. We are blessed when we walk with God." [14]

Our God Is Most Hospitable

The substance of God's heart is love. That love was profoundly exhibited at the cross. That love leads to God's gracious hospitality—an invitation and welcome into God's eternal home, an offer of salvation. So to teach the heart of God is to teach that God's love does lead people home. And since God wants everybody home, that love must be shared with all, within each generation. Who will do this except the body of Christ, his ambassadors? God's heart is beating with anticipation for you and your church. Hear it?

Hospitality Challenge

1. As you were growing up, did your family talk about faith and pass it on from one generation to another? Did family members reach beyond your home to others and reflect God's love upon them?
2. If you attended church frequently as a child, can you recall some of your best experiences from that tradition? Did anyone intentionally help you feel part of the family of faith? If yes, how did they?
3. If you did not attend church very often, do you remember someone inviting you to their church or introducing you to a God of love? If yes, what effect did that have on you?
4. What does it mean to surrender your *self* to God?
5. Which of God's love qualities are most difficult for you to emulate? Make an earnest effort to strengthen them in *your* list of love qualities.
6. Read the following scriptures, seeking to understand what God is teaching about *hospitality* in each one. Take short, simple notes as you go. After completing the scriptures, replay the lessons learned. What do you hear God saying to you and your church? Tell others.
   - Old Testament—Genesis 18:1–8; Deuteronomy 6:1–9; 1 Kings 17
   - Gospels—Luke 14:12–24; John 4:1–30; Matthew 22:34–46; 28:16–20
   - New Testament Churches—Acts 2:42–47; 2 Corinthians 5:11, 14–20; Ephesians 5:1–2

Guided Prayer

1. Hold the Bible, as you begin to pray. Consider all the faithful people who passed God's salvation story from generation to generation. Now thank God for every individual, tribe, church, and nation that followed the scriptures and lived their lives *so the next generation might know.*
2. Think about the people who were faithful to shower God's amazing love unto *you*: inviting, welcoming, including, teaching, or encouraging you to want and accept God's love for yourself. Thank God for such love, and then thank God for those who shared it with you.
3. Ask God the bold question: "With whom do you want me to share your love, so they too might come to know you?" (Consider friends, relatives, associates, neighbors.)
4. Sit quietly and be open to names that come to you. Write them down and put them in your Bible so you will see them and be reminded to answer your calling.

CHAPTER 5

Practicing Active Love: Every Christian Is a Minister

Beloved, let us love one another; for love is of God, and he who loves is born of God
and knows God. He who does not love does not know God; for God is love.
—1 John 4:7–8 (RSV)

Reverend Yohe, a gentle gray-haired man with a kindly manner, loved me and helped me experience another dimension of love in my early childhood. The sermons he preached on "Loving People into the Kingdom of God" did not touch my heart; his active love for me did. The congregation embraced his example and his teaching. I felt I was a real part of my church family. To this day, when I return to that church, I feel loved by the household of faith. Such acceptance in my preschool years continues to fuel my longing for others to find a warm and welcoming church environment where love helps people to see and enter the kingdom of God.

How blessed I am to have had a nuclear family, an extended family, and a church family to ground me in God's plan of love and hospitality intended for all people. I believe that is why God challenged me in seminary with a project thesis "The Church Learning to Extend Hospitality: To Each Other, to Guests, and to Strangers in Our Midst Including the Least and the Lost." God has called my attention to the many people who are missing so much life-shaping love.

A case in point was made by a minister giving a hospitality seminar:

I was unchurched because my parents moved. They had previously attended church and initially had looked for a new one. Unfortunately, they became discouraged because no one even talked to them when they visited. So they gave up, and to this day, they do not have a relationship with a church family. But when I went to a Christian setting at age 15, people reached out to me; I found friends who intentionally helped me to connect. [1]

If newcomers meet Christians in any setting, a scent of God's love should be the welcome gift, wrapped in a friendly greeting and a hint of love from the host. If the gift is missing, the newcomers may soon be also.

"If we do not show love to one another, the world has a right to question whether Christianity is true." [2] This profound statement, made by Presbyterian minister Francis Schaeffer over forty years ago, remains valid now as then. The reality is this: God expects every Christian, all who claim the name of Christ and acknowledge his ultimate love, to respond in love to others. "God is love. If we keep on loving others, we will stay one in our hearts with God and he will stay one with us" (1 John 4:16b CEV). Our own family is meant to be a nursery of love. Within a church family, it is important that we enrich our love for each other and imperative that we create a climate where God's love thrives in us and attracts others to come and inhale the love.

However, loving someone we don't want to love or don't know how to love is most difficult. In the novel *The Brothers Karamazov* by Dostoevsky, a wealthy woman asks an elderly monk how she can really know that God exists. The monk tells her that no explanation or argument can achieve this, only the practice of "active love."

The woman confides that sometimes she dreams about a life of loving service to others. She could become a Sister of Mercy, live in holy poverty, and serve the poor in the humblest ways. But then it occurs to her how ungrateful some people she would serve are likely to be. They would probably complain that the soup wasn't hot enough or the bread wasn't fresh or the bed was too hard. She confesses that she couldn't bear such ingratitude.

Her dreams about serving others vanish, and once again she finds herself wondering if there really is a God. To this the monk responds, "Love in practice is a harsh and dreadful thing compared to love in dreams." [3]

A very strong thread throughout the Bible assures that God's love will move us far beyond mere dreams. Though the way may appear harsh and dreadful, our journey is pioneered by the God of love. We who know God's love know peace, joy, and hope; those who don't know God's love might have no peace, joy, or hope. How terrible is that?

The scriptures below display a tapestry of God's love in action. The themes that are portrayed stretch from God's imposing love, to a look at what love is, to our expected response. They are sewn tightly together by the Holy Spirit within the verses. Reading them in their entirety will help us see afresh the wide spectrum and its patterns of God's love. May we become more inspired to pass it on.

- We are reminded of the many ways "God's faithful love lasts forever" (Psalm 136 CEB).
- Jesus prayed for his disciples: "Just as you sent me into the world, I am sending them into the world" (John 17:18, 21–22, 26 NLT).
- "Love is patient, kind … never gives up" (1 Corinthians 13:4, 7 NLT).
- "Imitate God, therefore, in everything you do … Live a life filled with love" (Ephesians 5:1–2 NLT)
- "And God has given us his Spirit as proof that" (1 John 4:13 NLT).

The Flow of Love

God is the source of a pure, steadfast, unconditional love poured into each created child. Some of our imperfections taint and obstruct the intended flow of God's love through us. When we, as believing Christians, drink in the sacrificial love of Jesus, our reservoir of love is purified. Then the Holy Spirit transforms us into channels of love that can flow more freely and with greater power. If we so choose, we can live out our love for God by loving people. We are not identified by the love God gives us; God loves everyone. Instead, the world will know we are Christians by the love we pour into the lives of others.

Just as the wealthy woman decided, living a life of love might not be so easy. Following the example of Christ may not be what we've dreamed. But when *we* become the object of Jesus' prayer in John 17, above, we will be filled with God's love overflowing into a desperate world that needs to believe.

Consider a four-tier fountain that continually fills up. Just for the taking, rivers of living water pour from God's heart into each of our beings. The water rises in us and overflows to family and friends and then tumbles to our church family and neighborhood community. From there, the living water of God cascades to the people beyond our churches and nearby communities; it reaches the world.[4]

A Fountain of Living Water

*... because God's love has been poured into our hearts
through the Holy Spirit which has been given to us.* (Rom. 5:5 RSV)

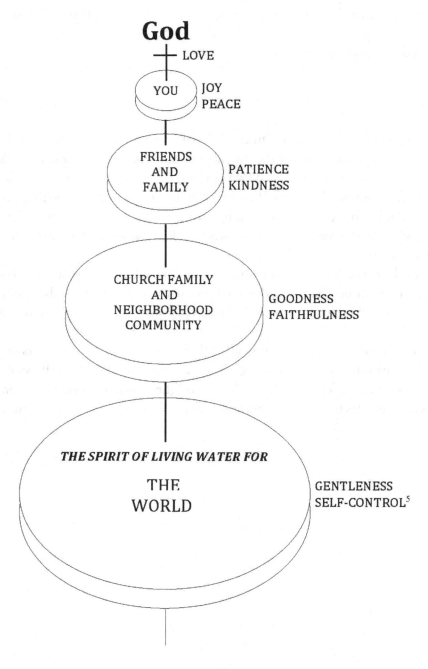

When our love for someone is sincere, all the fruit of the Spirit springs forth. Joy and peace shower both giver and receiver. Patience, kindness, goodness, faithfulness, gentleness, and self-control saturate the relationship.

God puts the capacity to love into every individual. Each provision of love is abundant. We must purposely channel it to awaken and help activate the love in others. Could it be that some individuals become spiritually ineffective, and some churches dwindle in size because the dream of practicing God's active love doesn't always reveal the rugged terrain of life?

As Dostoevsky's monk pointed out, the reality is often a difficult, seemingly overwhelming task. Getting up to feed or change a baby in the middle of the night, pouring yourself out to care for the sick or oppressed, and sharing the good news with those uneducated in the faith do not happen easily. We are reminded, however, that God does not intend for us to muster this love on our own. But we must be willing to face challenges and press on through tough times.

Our response should be similar to that of people in the first-century church who had received a vision of a life in Christ. Those early Christians were filled with awe! They were open to what God wanted to do *through* them, and they encountered the love of God in all its fullness by way of the Father, the Son, and the Holy Spirit. It occurred initially within their church community. In love, they were together to study and follow the scriptures in earnest; to live in fellowship as God's family; to worship and pray, seeking peace, strength, and common purpose. While maintaining accountability *and* encouragement, obeying God and loving one another began to surge. Love inside the church rose and spilled over to the outside. The tradition of God's hospitality had been set in motion. More and more people were invited to connect with the believers and learn of God's love. Newcomers were added and found faith in the triune God for themselves.[6]

God yearns for everyone to know and feel the divine love that was experienced and shared by the first Christian church. Marjorie Thompson defines our actively obedient roles as individuals and churches: "Hospitality is essentially an expression of love. It is a movement to include the guest in the very best of what we ourselves have received and can therefore offer."[7]

Hospitality *is* love in action. So how in the world do we start?

From Friendly to Friendships and Further

Being friendly is how we start. Hospitality requires a readiness to open kindly relations with folks outside our current circles, those who may differ considerably from us. A willingness to connect, welcoming the possibility of becoming a friend, is paramount. Friendliness should demonstrate real interest in a person. Chris Walker refers to this beginning stage in which we initiate relationships as "meaningful small talk."[8] As we continue to connect, we strengthen and expand our sphere of friendly relationships. Good and robust friendships may emerge. Such friendships need not be intimate but ones where conversation and caring persist.

Perhaps a fitting expression for engaging others in this way is *friendship evangelism*. That "E-word" is often unpopular because its practice at times is overzealous. In a new relationship, both people need time, patience, and understanding to know and be known by the other. To go from friendly to friendship takes trust. And when trust is strong, sharing the good news can be as natural as comparing favorite foods or headache remedies. Bits and pieces of God's love can find a way into conversations, enhanced by actions. We are to align with God's hope to make all human beings his friends through Christ.

Jesus, the Model Friend

While on this earth, Jesus was about making friends. He was accurately accused of eating with sinners.[9] Jesus called people to come be with him: the poor, the oppressed, the outcasts.[10] He referred to any who followed him not as servants but friends.[11] Ultimately, Jesus laid down his life for all who would become his friends.[12] When he returned to the Father, Jesus left the labor of kingdom building to them.[13] Jesus had taught and demonstrated that making friends is an avenue by which God conveys hospitality and leads people into the kingdom, no matter their present station in life.

For years the church has sung the well-loved hymn "What a Friend We Have in Jesus." From a contemporary genre, strains of "Jesus, Friend of Sinners" are lifted up. Yet we too often fail to appreciate and honor the messages within these hymns. My father had an innate understanding of the messages, and he accepted the biblical challenge to make friends. He would eagerly approach any newcomer, whether in church or out, and introduce meaningful small talk. *He never met a stranger.*

My friend Judy is a "friendship maker." This was acknowledged after her pastor asked her, along with a group of others, to share briefly in worship a prayerful vision for their church. She responded, "Some of you know I am a big fan of red-carpet hospitality. What if we could turn every visitor into a friend, assimilate them into friendship? That's what I am praying for. Let's all just take a little time to let that sink in."[14] Suppose everybody did—and then acted upon it. What might the result be?

Friendships for Every Season of a Soul

While in conversation with Todd, a man forty years old and recently released from prison, I was struck by a reference he made to his bad choices: "It was like my thinking was frozen, and I couldn't get out."

I smiled, and these words came out of my mouth: "It was like your soul was in winter, but now it is starting to thaw. That's God who was there all the time, trying to get through. As you recognize that, you are giving God permission to come in and warm your heart." I happen to know it was the love and friendship of several people in a congregation that contributed to the change in Todd's heart.

Before his release, these folks bought a book intended to help him discover God's love and purpose for his life. Since no books could be sent to the prison, they tore the book into separate pages and divided it among themselves. Coordinating their efforts, sequential pages were included with letters mailed to Todd. These innovative people, whose souls were in a warmer season, produced love to share with their incarcerated friend. They were laboring for a harvest that would bear much fruit.

A wonderful part of the story is that Todd loved the book and talked about it with his prison mates. If they wanted to read it, he would barter with them for candy bars. Good news travels in unusual ways. My experience with Todd has helped me to consider that people have "seasons" in their spiritual lives. When we can determine what season they are in, we know better how to love them.

> *Winter*: While the seed of our soul holds the nature of God within, our frigid response to God's love and warmth keeps our love trapped inside a frozen heart. God determined, "Let's create humans in our likeness." But because of free choice, humanity has fallen into sin and refuses to rejoin God's desire for a right relationship with us. When our hearts are frozen, we deny God or choose a replacement, even ourselves. Yet despite our rebellion, God still pursues us with love. God does not abandon souls in winter; neither should we.

> *Spring*: The sun and rain upon the good earth can quietly dawn new life and draw it toward the sky. In like manner, God silently plants seeds in human hearts with hope they will germinate into new life and love. This spiritual awakening may even happen without our being aware. The poet penned this as "The Hound of Heaven."[15] John Wesley referred to this preceding, persistent love as "prevenient grace."[16] It is God abounding in steadfast love, just as promised throughout the scriptures, most clearly at work from our conception to conversion. This spiritual season is a new dawn gently springing warm impulses that can thaw rigid attitudes. It is the Master Planner drawing us to accept for ourselves the relationship God offers us in Christ.

> *Summer*: When we consciously open our hearts to the unconditional love of God, made known in all its fullness, we meet Christ Jesus personally. As we entrust our lives to a new beginning of forgiveness, rebirth, and the reassurance of God's presence, love takes root in our lives, and we begin to bloom and grow. The Bible refers to this as being justified.[17] Scriptures remind us that Jesus Christ justifies us before God. It is "just as if we have never sinned." Our hearts are strangely warmed

by embracing this amazing salvation gift; we know the love of Christ which passes knowledge, and are filled with fullness of God. We become a new creation and want others to experience this as well.

Harvest Time: This season is expansive; it is meant to endure. Once we have embraced Jesus, who has made us right in the eyes of God, we enter the kingdom of God, striving to live as God's righteous people. We then push on toward reattaining the likeness of God. Before going to the cross, knowing he was leaving his disciples and in deep agonizing love, Jesus prayed, "Sanctify them in truth, your word is truth" (John 17:17 NRSV). Jesus wanted his disciples to take in God's goodness and truth for themselves and to constantly grow into the holiness of God. The apostle Paul referred to such accountability and quest as *sanctification*. It is the fulfillment of Jesus' teaching: to learn "the kingdom of God is within you". (Luke 17:20–21 NIV).

But there was more to Jesus' prayer: "As you have sent me into the world, so I have sent them into the world … Righteous Father … the love with which you have loved me may be in them, and I in them" (John 17:18, 25a, 26b NRSV). Jesus also taught his disciples. "The harvest is plentiful, but the laborers are few" (Luke 10:2 NRSV). He then prayed that they would adopt the mandate to reap souls for God's kingdom.

Both of Jesus' prayers were not just for the disciples but for all who believe in him. So we who have taken on a new life in Christ are on the path to sanctification. If we remain faithful, the journey will lead us to acquiring the likeness of God. And since God wants a great harvest of new believers to take up residence in the kingdom, God tells us the job is ours. Yes, we are called to make disciples of Jesus Christ to transform the world. What a harvest that will be!

Perhaps you or someone you know needs to experience hope and God's love in a new season. The truth of these words from the song "At the Cross" might help:

> Oh, Lord, You've searched me, You know my ways.
> Even when I fail You, I know You love me.
> Your holy presence, surrounding me in every season,
> I know You love me, I know You love me.[18]

What a profound thought—in every season of our souls, we are loved and loved and loved.

Love Requires a Response

God's steadfast, unconditional love for all humankind has endured forever! It is the standard by which our love for another, including God, is measured. Loving all others is the response required for the love God gives each of us. It is not easy to measure up.

Many of us were blessed to be surrounded by human love from birth. We entered a world of parents, grandparents, and extended family who met our physical and emotional needs. Feeding, clothing, holding, and kissing us was love in action. When we stepped into the broader world of neighbors, teachers, and church leaders, we were often made to feel special, drawn into a circle of love. Then, having accepted the love from others and having had those good feelings, we gradually learned some truth about love: we could make others feel good by actively loving them in return; we could even love them *first*. This is the response God wants from all who have *ever* been shown love! God always intended love to be a two-way street, but in a broken world, roadblocks and potholes seem to be everywhere.

Those of us who embark upon a commitment to a special person soon discover that love has peaks and valleys. Being in a relationship that marries two lives into one can become the best of times or the worst of times. Keeping such a union strong doesn't just happen. It takes a continual exchange of love declared in many ways. And over a lengthy journey, the love will change. I didn't say diminish, although it can; I said change, which may make it even better. These changing times and ideas of love given and love received were programmed into our aging process when we were created. Don't be disheartened along the way. God is good at removing roadblocks and patching potholes.

Most prospective parents are afforded the luxury of loving their children even before they hold them in their arms. However, actively loving an infant or toddler, a teen or adult, a son or daughter requires sacrifice. God calls us to love our children even when we don't feel like it. That's part of our expected response for being God's beloved children. And as we imitate God's steadfast, unconditional love for our children, God teaches two lessons: (1) our children are learning what real love looks like and how to respond in like manner; and (2) we parents are learning that true, active love for anyone requires sacrifice—whether that love is accepted or not, returned or not. My husband frequently said, "One of the greatest effects of having children is that it teaches you to be unselfish." By the way, these lessons are available whether you are or aren't a parent. They are found within God's Text.

Refusal Is a Response

Every single one of us was created to live in love throughout a timeless existence. But both human love and divine love may be refused. Free choice given by God and evil influence inserted by Satan can make actively loving others very difficult—yet so vitally important. Perhaps you have loved someone for a long time, but that person still has not fully seized your love or God's love and forgiveness. You are tired and discouraged. Maybe you begin to doubt the power of love. Stop! Take a deep breath. God is in this with you. God continues to love you and the one you are struggling to love. Pray for strength and guidance. *Don't give up on loving.*

A host of people have never received love or have received only shallow expressions of it. Consider Mikie, the tough little guy who came to visit Paul and Ruby. The springtime of his precious but hurting soul was awakened to God's love while in their home. He did not refuse love; he invited it. But it had been a long winter.

Possibly you can identify with Mikie to some extent. You may readily need to be accepted and loved. You may need a good friend. Jesus wants to be your friend. They don't come any better; he laid down his life for his friends. Jesus will walk with you through every season of your soul. The more intimate you become with Jesus, the more hope and love you will receive and then be able to share with others. *Don't give up on being loved.*

The World Needs Love … Every Church, God's Agency

To effectively practice active love, we must stay connected to the source of love; we must become fruit-bearing branches of the vine. Jesus is very clear on the importance of doing so.[19] Although our connection to Jesus may be strong, we might not always feel like loving others. But we can't simply submit to our feelings; they don't have the final say. Love, support, and encouragement flow to us through fellow Christians. In communion with the Spirit, we are refreshed, and we are counseled. We *can* continue.

The world is Jesus' mission field. We honor our friendship with him by becoming his coworkers. We help Jesus minister to our families, neighborhoods, schools, and workplaces. We become agents of God, actively loving others wherever we are.

The Christian church is the only institution in the world that proclaims the kind of love that includes forgiveness and reconciliation. Unfortunately, far too many churches have not seen anyone become a new believer in Christ for years. No one has been welcomed into God's kingdom. Yet the number continues to increase for the people who have little or no understanding of God's great love.

I once read a news article about a survey in Europe that indicated 98 percent of the people do not attend a church. They apparently visit their cathedrals primarily to observe the beauty. My visits there tend to confirm that conclusion. One Sunday morning, my husband and I caught a cab, and we directed the driver to take us to the cathedral. He replied, "The tours don't start until 1:00 p.m." When we said we wanted to attend worship, he was very surprised. Bells ring, people enter, but only a few worship.

We would like to think the United States is doing much better than Europe with church attendance. Well, we need to learn some facts. The 2008 United Methodist General Conference reported that 80 percent of the people in the USA have no meaningful relationship with a church. So who is responsible for helping that 80 percent experience the fullness of God's love?

Here are some shocking statistics noted from a workshop,
"Why Nobody Wants to Go to Church Anymore"

- Over a period of years, more than four thousand churches closed their doors annually.
- Church attendance is shrinking. While 40 percent of Americans say they attend church every week, the actual number is more like 20 percent.
- The percent of congregations characterized by *high spiritual vitality* dropped from about 43 percent in 2005 to 28 percent in 2010.
- In just five years, the percentage of teenagers attending church every week went from 20 percent to 15 percent.
- For some time, 2.7 million church members had fallen into inactivity yearly.
- From 1990 to 2000, the combined membership of all Protestant denominations in the US declined by almost five million, or 9.5 percent, while the US population increased by 24 million, or 11 percent.
- Half of all churches in the US did not add any new members to their ranks between 2010 and 2013.
- Researchers are predicting that by 2020, more than 85 percent of Americans won't worship God at church. [20]

Fast forward five years. The newest research from Thom S. Rainer confirms the swift-moving, stark reality of the Schultz report above. Studies released in 2018 cite that in recent years six thousand to ten thousand churches have closed their doors. On a weekly tabulation, one hundred to two hundred congregations discover they can no longer continue ministering to their dwindling church family. With 150 congregations disbanding weekly, that is an average of nearly eight thousand annually. The report ends with a hopeful thought: "Churches have always been asleep before an awakening." We need an awakening! [21]

Such research results should startle us to pray and then obey: "Lord, show us your way. Make us effective; awaken us to be active agents of your love."

The Lord's Way of Love

As Christians, we have been shown God's way. It goes through the cross. God's love for all led to the cross; Christ's love for all leads beyond the cross. We are to love all as we are loved. In our churches, such love must include *radical hospitality* extended to everyone, members and nonmembers. Being genuine and humble, we should be willing to develop relationships even with people unlike ourselves. Remember that "every saint has a past, and every sinner has a future."[22] Christians are simply the conduits through which Christ's love flows.

Jesus tells his friends: "Remain in me, and I will remain in you ... As the Father has loved me, so have I loved you. Remain in my love ... My command is this: Love each other as I have loved you" (John 15:4, 9, 12 NIV). We cannot give what we do not have. Staying connected to Christ is how we receive love. And when we make a conscious effort to love others, that connection opens for Christ to love them through us. That's how we love the one who loved us first.

In conversation with a Young Life leader, I heard this story: Paul was a Young Life camp counselor. Among his campers was a young, rebellious guy, determined to make life as miserable as possible for his counselor. Night after night, he plotted to disrespect and make fun of him. Night after night, Paul was reinforced by God with an inpouring of patience, wisdom, and love. While still maintaining the necessary level of control, Paul reached out in love to this *unlovable* one.

At the ending of camp, each camper was given the opportunity to openly describe what a Christian is to look like. The devious teen, who had created all kinds of havoc, only to be loved in spite of it, called out the name Paul.

Paul had understood and acted upon another truth: the more unlovable a person may seem, the more human love that person needs. This selfless love floats as a pleasant aroma. Even the "difficult" camper caught the fragrance of Christ in the love Paul had shown. "They'll know we are Christians by our love."[23] Every Christian is a minister, inside and outside the church. Love preaches!

Hospitality Challenge

1. Do the statistics regarding fewer and fewer people attending church alarm you? Why or why not?
2. Consider how much the members of your church love each other.
   a. Rate your church from 1 to 10: 1 for "not much at all" and 10 for "very much."
   b. Do you believe your rating affects how much those outside are attracted to your church?
   c. If so, to what extent?
3. Answer the following in *one short* sentence: How do we show love to the one who loved us first?
4. As for folks who have very little in common with us, going from making friends to actively loving them can require passing through rough areas on the relationship journey. We must continue forward by connecting, conversing, and caring.
   a. What other ways could help us earn and keep a person's trust?
   b. As Christian "ministers," how should we respond to people we love when they are clearly ungrateful?
   c. How can we help someone become justified before God?

Prayer for Myself

Loving God, remind me once again, that you are the author of *all* love. When I feel love, and when I offer love, you are the source. May I never act like one who does not know that you *are* love, and you *are* amazing power. Bring your love into each relationship I have. And let that demonstrate your use of people to bring love into the lives of others. Amen and amen.

Prayer for My Church

And now, Lord, I am praying for our church. Forgive us for not caring for—in fact writing off—those who have lost their way; those who don't know of your love; or those who have become hardened by circumstances of life. Forgive us for being better at judging than loving. Show us how to become a church that really surrenders to your will for bringing others into your kingdom. Remind us to depend upon the love of Christ to urge us on. Amen.

PART III

Who Is Called to Extend God's Hospitality?

Every Christian and Every Faction of the Church

CHAPTER 6

What's a Church to Do? Overflow with Love, Hope, and Power

Welcome one another, therefore, just as Christ has welcomed you, for the glory of God.
—Romans 15:7 (NRSV)

I once heard someone refer to ineffective and powerless Christians. Too often we are, as Eleanor Roosevelt is alleged to have said, like a teabag; we don't know how strong we are until we're in hot water! I believe that analogy is true. As Christians, we have a resurrection power that comes into our lives as a free gift. Frequently unaware that such a gift is accessible, many do not seek it. But the Holy Spirit's power is there for the taking. Jesus said, "You will receive power when the Holy Spirit comes upon you" (Acts 1:8a NLT).

Sadly, some churches are dwindling and dying because they have not pursued this power. Many, by side-stepping any hot water, have lost their way to advancing the kingdom of God. But for those who do receive this power, Jesus said, "And you will be my witnesses, telling people about me everywhere" (Acts 1:8b NLT). God's power is to flow through our churches. invigorating believers to help others get on and stay on the path to the kingdom. Designing a plan to provide hospitality and inviting others to experience God's love are in true accord with God's purpose. A church that steps out in faith, steeping itself in the living water of Christ, will not get burned. Instead, it will absorb the kind of courage and power found in the first Christian church and be ready to engage in God's plan.

A hospitality plan runs throughout the scriptures. God, the Creator and Host, chose the people of Israel to live in his redeeming love and to demonstrate that love to the rest of the world. Welcoming the stranger became a solidly established Hebrew tradition. To be certain, the Old Testament hospitality practice of embracing the stranger is difficult for us; it goes against our

American culture. We live in a privatized world, having much independent housing, extensive personal transportation, and our own ethnic ways. We keep the circle of people with whom we trustingly connect relatively small. Moving beyond family, friends, coworkers, or others like us can seem too uncomfortable.

Community Life Has Changed

At one time in America, neighborhood life happened on the front porch and community life at the general store. Families helped each other; resources were shared. When children got in trouble, neighbors served as parental figures. A feeling of family emitted throughout much of the community. Gradually, this way of life began to change as families and individuals became more and more self-reliant. Neighbors do not know each other by name. Strangers are feared, not welcomed. As a result, our churches have often become settings of *like* people. Rather than invite and include outsiders, we unconsciously (or consciously) hope that anyone not like us will stay away.

National Life Has Changed

Early pilgrims relocated to America seeking freedom to worship God without adhering to a government church. In writing the United States constitution, the framers established freedom of religion by prohibiting a single government church. Principals for living together were: one nation, permitting personal and public acknowledgments of God, with liberty and justice for all. Engraved government buildings, printed money, creeds, military chaplains and public prayers openly justified Judeo-Christian theology within the foundation of America.

Cultural shifts now exist within contemporary society. Established religious bodies, as well as other faiths, and people of no faith currently contribute loose, individualized interpretations of *separation of church and state*. Public expressions of faith, even worshipping together can be costly. As Christians, navigating such uncertain and muddied waters, we struggle. We pray, "Thy kingdom come, Thy will be done on earth as it is in heaven" yet relate and welcome others tentatively into God's Kingdom.

In the midst of ambiguity and confusion, we certainly continue to exercise our constitutional rights of freedom of speech and freedom of religion. However, a question arises: Are we willing to live out Jesus' message of sacrificial love and redemption, or do we just want to declare it? Despite rising cultural resistance to faith, the Apostle Paul would remind us, "the fruit of the Spirit is love, joy, peace, longsuffering, kindness, goodness, faithfulness, gentleness, self-control. Against such there is no law." (Galatians 5:22-23 NKJV). Christians, and the gathered church remain called to impact our nation and world today!

Christian Church Life *Must* Change

Many churches have veered from God's intended path. Current pursuits do not properly represent Jesus' vision for the kingdom. We must relearn God's plan for God's world and rediscover the ground rules laid out for those of us who claim to be the people of God.

A new look at how God welcomes people into the kingdom is imperative. Author Bishop Robert Schnase, overseer of hundreds of congregations, challenges us with his definition of Christian hospitality:

> Christian hospitality refers to the active desire to invite, welcome, receive, and care for those who are strangers so that they find a spiritual home and discover for themselves the unending richness of life in Christ. It describes genuine love for others who are not yet part of the faith.[1]

We belong to the body of Christ because of another's hospitality. Someone invited us, encouraged us, received us, and helped us feel welcome—a parent, spouse, friend, pastor, or even a stranger. Practicing God's hospitality within the church congregation is decisively important.

Schnase continues:

> Christian hospitality is the lifeline of the Body of Christ … Vibrant, fruitful, growing congregations practice radical hospitality. Out of genuine love for Christ and others, their laity and pastors take the initiative to invite, welcome, include, and support newcomers; helping them grow in faith … Hospitality is a mark of Christian discipleship. It shows people that God in Christ values them and loves them.[2]

Other researchers see hospitality practices as essential to bringing newcomers into the kingdom of God. Note that *hospitality* appears in both of the following lists by Jeffrey D. Wilson and Albert L. Winseman:

The Baker's Dozen of Church Growth

1. Spirituality
2. Pastor
3. *Hospitality* (emphasis added)
4. Flexibility
5. Exciting worship
6. Lay leadership
7. Quality care and nurture

8. Intentional assimilation
9. New small groups
10. Community outreach
11. Building and grounds
12. Marketing
13. Visitor follow-up[3]

Healthy Congregations Have Member Expectations

1. Commit to spiritual growth
2. Commit to worshipping with others
3. Commit to financial support
4. Commit to the congregation's mission and vision
5. Commit to the needs of the community and world
6. *Commit to hospitality* (emphasis added)
7. Commit to prayer[4]

Hospitality Is a Spiritual Discipline

Every Christian should exercise the spiritual discipline of hospitality as faithfully as they worship, commune, study the Bible, and pray. Hospitality to God is finally expressed in our intentions and actions toward every creature God loves. We are not permitted to separate our love for God from our love for others.[5]

It should come as no surprise that churches that do not practice hospitality are shrinking and dying. Churches thrive because they enact God's hospitality. As Christians, however, we must extend hospitality beyond our desire to thrive. Hospitality is pivotal to the meaning of the gospel; it's about following Jesus. Christine Pohl writes, "As the Biblical texts on hospitality are lived out, and as the Scriptures illumine and interpret present practices, Christians find their lives infused with the presence of Christ."[6] There is no greater spiritual discipline than a practice that enables us to sense the nearness of Christ. Such an experience prompts and urges us to patiently and lovingly lead others to feel that Christ is here—with them!

Dreaming What a Congregation Can Do

As for advancing the kingdom of God, hospitality is a component in each formula derived by Schnase, Wilson, or Winseman. There is strong evidence that any dream of growing a congregation must contain an element of extending hospitality. To accomplish the dream requires vision and determination, both instilled by the Spirit of God. If we then start practicing the habits of the first Christian church, we begin fulfilling God's Word:

> In the last days, God says, "I will pour out my Spirit on all people.
>
> Your sons and daughters will prophesy, your young men will see visions, your old men will dream dreams." … And each day the Lord added to their fellowship those who were being saved. (Acts 2:17, 47 NIV)

Selling the Hospitality Ministry

If a church desires for biblical hospitality to channel through all that the church does, it is necessary to see and develop a vision. Visioning is a process that seeks to have the entire staff and congregation come aboard. This is a formidable objective that requires support and input from the full church leadership and needs to be bathed in much prayer. Once the vision has been created, developed, documented, and ultimately approved, it must be thoroughly disseminated and carefully taught. Every ministry of the church must embrace its practices.

Most certainly, there will be a need for many more of the congregation to invest in this ministry. The pastor and leadership must sell the importance of that investment and the vitality of the ministry. God's hospitality in the church hinges upon it.

Best Practices for a Ministry of Hospitality

Every congregation should take the following general ideas and personalize them to meet their specific circumstances:

1. Church staff and members must be committed to practice active love. Their efforts should be deliberate, both inside and outside the walls of the church, seeking innovative avenues to express the invitation, "Come experience God's love." A few friendly people cannot create a hospitable church. It calls for the entire church to be alert for those readily in need of love.

2. The congregation must present a welcoming, loving, and caring environment. This setting will sustain opportunity for both the guest and the host to experience God's love. Such an environment will give the Holy Spirit occasion to touch and transform hearts. The church must review long-standing policies and practices that may be counter to these hopes. Then ask, "Who is not coming because they do not feel comfortable in the church?" Leadership must be sensitive to this question and work toward keeping church policy newcomer-friendly.

3. The congregation must have a heart for those without faith. "Jesus said that his driving passion was to 'seek out and save the lost.' If that was Jesus' driving passion, it must be the driving passion in our churches," says Adam Hamilton.[7] While the word *lost* is seldom used in our current church culture, we realize so many people are unaware of the transforming love and forgiveness Jesus offers.

4. The congregation cannot expect those unfamiliar with the church to act or live as Christians. Some behaviors of those who will come to our churches need to be overlooked. Jesus did not expect people to clean up their acts before they came to him. As Christians, we are to follow Jesus' example: "to love them as we find them, or as they may become."[8] There must be space for grace. In fishing for new believers, it is the disciple's role to catch the fish and God's role to clean them.

5. A hospitality plan must be in place and diligently followed. In providing hospitality, specific people doing specific tasks are to be firmly set. Determine how you will identify and welcome newcomers. Greeters, ushers, pew hosts, parking lot attendants, welcome-center hosts, attendance registrars, persons giving gifts and literature, and those doing follow-up must know and perform their special duties. Also, members in the pews should go out of their way to connect with newcomers.

6. The church's hospitality must include ministry *with*—not simply *to*—the poor. We cannot be the church of Jesus Christ, embracing salvation each day of forever, without including the poor. They are to be involved as active members in the body of Christ. However, much care and planning is crucial in creating the manner of ministry with the poor; it must accommodate their station in life. No one should feel overwhelmed or out of place. No one should be excluded. God is available to everyone, the poor included. Over two thousand verses in scripture say so.

7. The church building and its surroundings are to be clean, attractive, and functional. Evaluate the attendee-friendliness of the church facility—convenient parking; appealing grounds; clear walkways; disabled accessibility; doors clearly marked as an entrance or not, with appropriate directional signs both outside and inside; a spacious welcome center; safe and pleasant childcare areas; very clean restrooms; and clutter-free entryways, tables, shelves, classrooms. Look as if you are expecting visitors.

So What *Is* a Church to Do?

A congregation wanting to be abundantly alive and wanting to grow the kingdom of God must practice radical hospitality. It demands a deep spiritual commitment to follow the ways of Jesus, who welcomes all. And fundamentally, this may require change in attitudes, core values, and objectives that are currently lived out in many of our faith communities.

In a Catholic church, while attending a funeral, I read their creed and was told by a member that they begin every mass with this creed:

> We are Corpus Christi, the Body of Christ. We are His hands to reach out, His eyes to see, His ears to listen, His voice to share His love. Each of us has a gift to give and with Your help, O God, I will be friendly. I will be holy. I will do Your work. I will be prayerful. I will be generous. I will invite others to worship. I will be loyal and loving, faithful and compassionate, charitable and merciful. With Your help, O God, I will unite my gifts with those of others to strengthen the Body of Christ, Corpus Christi. Amen.[9]

In a sermon by the pastor of a Presbyterian church, proclaiming the gospel of God's hospitality, were these words: "A Savior who welcomes all, those shut out and excluded and those who follow, creates the community of the church where everyone of every race and condition has a place, a home."[10]

If we really want to know what a church is to do:
Imitate God.
Yearn for people.
Be open to people.
Love people.
Practice hospitality with all people.

Whenever we invite, bring, welcome, include, encourage, and involve, we help them belong. That *is* hospitality. "God has put eternity into the hearts of people" (Ecclesiastes 3:11). The task of a church is to introduce them to God's eternal hospitality, and help lead them home, where they would dwell with God—now and forever.

Hospitality Challenge

1. Consider the title "What's a Church to Do?" Without looking back at the chapter, try these:
   a. Write three answers to the question using four words or fewer in each of your answers.
   b. Write one answer having seven to twelve words.
   c. Share your answers aloud.
2. Contemplate the meaning of "radical hospitality." Still no peeking. Then discuss its attributes and descriptions that are so important to Christ's churches.
3. It's okay now to return to the chapter.
   a. Thoughtfully review the list of Best Practices.
   b. Pray over the list, asking God, "What do you want *our* church to do?"
   c. If you are a layperson, and God nudges you, seek out a friend (or more) in your congregation who may have been nudged likewise. Talk and pray together about where God might be leading you. Then go talk with the pastor.
   d. If you are a pastor, preach a sermon on "God's Heart for Hospitality." Seek feedback from several people who have responded in a positive way.
   e. Keep praying for the Spirit of God to blow throughout your church, breathing life into your hope to imitate God's hospitality.

Prayer

Savior, who welcomes all, help me to recognize that life is great because it is filled with great opportunities to love you by caring for people. Help us, as a church, to overflow with love, hope, and power. Help those who are not part of your church sense that *our* caring is really *your* love for them. Show us what our church is to do. Amen.

CHAPTER 7

Let a Team Begin: Reflecting God's Heart

Don't just pretend to love others, really love them ... work hard and serve
the Lord enthusiastically. Always be eager to practice hospitality.
—Romans 12:9, 11, 13 (NLT)

The young church in Rome read the letter—more direction from their mentor, Paul: *Don't pretend to love; have genuine affection for each other ... work hard in serving the Lord ... be patient with others ... help those in need ... Stay eager to practice hospitality!* The apostle was teaching the church to live out what Jesus taught his disciples: "Just as I have loved you, you should love each other. Your love for one another will prove to the world that you are my disciples" (John 13:34–35 NLT). Paul necessitates a heartiness to practice hospitality on all levels:

Each other—a congregation that does not extend love and hospitality to each other is not likely to draw outsiders to their church.

Visitors and guests—emphasis must be given to those not yet part of the family.

The least and the lost—they may differ from us, tending to have fewer resources, a certain lack of decorum, and a more limited knowledge of God, especially how to live out their beliefs. We who have received God's grace are mandated to help restore those who have not yet known and experienced that amazing grace. Real love seeks out and enthusiastically welcomes, invites, and brings others into the family setting.

Catching the Congregation's Attention—the Good, the Bad, and the Lesson

Early on, to create a more hospitable atmosphere, it is essential *to do something visible* to help the congregation see we are eagerly practicing hospitality. A contemporary author Nelson Searcy offers such a specific hospitality practice. He pointedly writes, "While it would be easy to let your guests fend for themselves to find a seat, it's a terrible idea."[1] So we begin with a new custom: for newcomers to our worship services, we offer to usher them to their seats.

Newcomers are often nervous when coming into a church for the first time. They need a greeting that reassures them of being both welcome and wanted. Assigned greeters and ushers are given opportunity to make that happen. An easy way to start is walking with folks to their seats. This also affords time for brief conversations, initiating relationships. A combination of two greeters and one usher at each entry point and having interchangeable roles is apt to work well, even when the number of attendees is large. A hospitality team plans and oversees this practice.

Jean was looking for a church to call home. Upon entering one on her search, she was delighted to have a greeter approach her, saying, "Welcome to our church. My name is Sandy." Jean immediately responded with her name. When Sandy accompanied her to the worship area, Jean said, "Thank you for helping me find a place. I wouldn't want to sit in someone else's seat." Her concern about taking *another's seat* should never need to come to mind. Although reserving seats for late-arriving family, friends, or guests may be acceptable, laying claim to seats already occupied is not.

Ethan had been absent from a particular church for several years. His marriage, entire family life, and job were crumbling. One Sunday, he and his wife slipped in, perhaps hopeful of a new beginning. A few minutes after they had sat down, a member walked to the pew and declared, "You're sitting in my seat." It immediately produced anger and embarrassment. A horrible way to treat anyone, but for a couple struggling, it was devastating—Ethan never came back. He and his wife divorced, and she moved on to another church. Might this string of events have an eternal effect upon Ethan? Unfortunately, yes!

Hopefully, what Ethan and his wife experienced will help to educate entire congregations: no one *owns* a seat in God's house except God, and God shares. We are to eagerly and readily carry out God's common love, beginning with common courtesy. Until God's example of hospitality becomes common throughout a congregation, the church will remain vulnerable to selfish ownership behavior—on several levels.

A Call to Action

Nearly twenty years before I started this book, I diligently took on the work to find the meaning of God's hospitality as part of a doctoral of ministry program. I invited a covenant group of twelve people from my local congregation to embark on part of the journey with me. We met in my home regularly, studied scriptures on hospitality, prayed, and worked through an engaging faith-sharing hospitality book.[2] Our group invested in self-reflection. We grappled with the questions below. Other than number 6, *we* meant the group members.

1. In whose house do we worship?
2. How are we hospitable to each other?
3. How are we hospitable to visitors?
4. How are we hospitable to people in the neighborhood?
5. How are we in this together?
6. How do we, the church, show appreciation for being guests in the neighborhood? Most of us who attend drive to the church. The neighborhood consists of those who live there.

Here are a few statements recorded as God's hospitality was awakening in our souls:

1. We are hospitable to those we know personally.
2. I believe the church is the Lord's house, but I don't believe it's seen by strangers as a public place.
3. We must be organized; more needs to be done in the ways of welcoming visitors.
4. We need to do more to personally invite others, to say things like "Come with me; sit with me."
5. Keep the right-of-way *open* through the church with a convincing welcome mat.
6. I sense that not all members of the congregation share the vision. Some would like to "keep things in the family." How do we help them catch the vision? It's a tough, complex task.
7. *All* need to come to know Jesus. How can we increase their coming?

Moving Beyond Friendly

Part of a note from a woman in the group, whose eyes were lifted to new heights of hospitality within the church, shows how God was working in her life:

> I have found it quite interesting to ponder the meaning of hospitality. It has always been my desire to be a hospitable person, and I strive to make guests in my home comfortable and do everything I can to practice hospitality at home. I never really pondered hospitality to one another at church but have tried to be a friendly person to others. Hospitality requires much more.

When one considers hospitality within the church, we realize that it must be a deliberate act that we set out to accomplish. Just being friendly isn't enough. We are a "family" within the church, a body of believers, and when you really consider the impact that we can make on one another's lives, you realize the importance of hospitality to one another.

As I reread Peggy's note, I renewed my prayer that this book might be helpful in some way for your church to expand God's family in your congregation.

Setting a Compass

Peggy now understood: being friendly is good, but that is only part of the package God intends hospitality to be. It requires caring, listening, compassion, and going out of our way for the *other*— loving those with whom we disagree, people without faith, complete strangers, and the unlikeable.

Responsibilities of a hospitality ministry develop from the need to replace divisive cultural habits and misguided beliefs with God's principles for bringing others into the kingdom. The covenant group, thinking in this direction, decided the best first move was to plan a hospitality event, personally inviting every member of the congregation. Here, hospitality would be experienced as well as taught. We were becoming a team. (See Appendix 1.)

These are the preparation and production steps we took:

- We sent an attractive written invitation to *every person* connected with the church.
- We continued a huge promotion—digital, bulletin, poster, and verbal announcements.
- We gave personal "Sit at my table" invitations; everyone likes to feel wanted.
- Each team member was expected to fill one or more tables.
- Each table had a host to welcome folks and lead directed activities.
- We planned a fun, upbeat, engaging program in which people could connect.
- Place cards with scriptures about hospitality facilitated focused table talk.
- All music, skits, or jokes intended to teach God's hospitality were to be well rehearsed.
- Laughter is invigorating. Examples of bad or no hospitality were included throughout the evening.
- We evaluated our church's current hospitality status with a test. Names were optional.
- At each table, we briefly discussed any surprises discovered from the test results.
- We collected the tests for the fledgling hospitality team to evaluate. (See Appendix 2.)

Build a Team—Grow God's Grace

God's hospitality is meant to be a ministry of every Christian and every church. Hopefully, you are becoming excited about such a ministry. Who is God bringing to mind as good candidates for the team? Seek the pastor's counsel and support. But the onus, the hard work of planning and implementing hospitality, rests on the team. The extent to which God's hospitality becomes "pervasive" depends greatly upon the agreement and assistance of *the ministers in the pews*. The team's and church's biggest mission is to educate and anoint the congregation. True hospitality runs through all that the church does.

Your church's unique culture and store of resources will help determine how you fashion your vision and fit your plan into God's design, found in scripture. The path trod by our original covenant group and team is not a necessity, but seeking and following the way God leads is most imperative. As your God-directed team and plan evolve, stay the course—model hospitality, teach and encourage your congregation to sincerely practice it, and then watch grace grow. God's love will show.

One new team began by developing a mission statement for their purposeful work: "Enfolding people into the loving arms of Christ, through association with God's people; for where hospitality is present, Christ is present."[3]

Structuring the Hospitality Team—Identify and Delegate Responsibilities

A hospitality team functions best when specific needed ministries within the overall mission are recognized and assigned to separate sub-teams. Leaders of sub-teams are to recruit people capable of serving the particular ministry well. This requires considering a person's prominent attributes: skills and abilities, interests and desires, personal limitations, busyness of schedule. Nearly everyone who has a heart for God's hospitality can be trained to do an important task for the team.

Many sub-team responsibilities, such as being greeters, ushers, or hosts, are inherent to most churches. (They are discussed in chapter 8.) Here are a few others that may meet or increase your mission needs: placing hospitality materials throughout the church, providing receptions, assisting at funerals, writing an appealing paragraph to newcomers, and connecting with regular attenders who have been absent for too long.

Cost or Investment?

The various ministries of the team do incur expenses. A budget is necessary for informational, invitational, and inspirational literature; welcome gifts; food and related supplies; some furniture for new spaces of welcome; and miscellaneous minor expenditures. But the bottom line is miniscule compared to what is redeemed. The largest outlays are time, energy, and love, given by the dedicated hospitality teammates who help a church become God's church for all.

God's Place of Welcome
Build Wide Its Portals

Step Up Your Prayer Power:

> Don't worry about anything, instead pray about everything. Tell God what you need, and thank him for all he has done. Then you will experience God's peace, which exceeds anything we can understand. His peace will guard your hearts and minds as you live in Christ Jesus. (Philippians 4:6–8 NLT)

We, as Christians of all ages, have the task of reconciling people to God. Being hospitable is not just something we do; it is something we become. So as a team, we pray to become more hospitable. Prayer stirs God's love in our hearts. Intimacy with God results in intimacy with humanity.[4]

The poet penned it well: "More things are wrought by prayer than the world dreams of."[5]

In hope, we pray, "Lord, mold us to work well together, helping others to connect with you." The eternal results will be more than we dreamed.

Step Up Your Organization and Education:

> In his grace, God has given us different gifts for doing certain things well … If your gift is serving others, serve them well. If you are a teacher, teach well … If your gift is to encourage others, be encouraging. If it is giving, give generously. If God has given you leadership ability, take the responsibility seriously. And if you have a gift for showing kindness to others, do it gladly. (Romans 12:6–8 NLT)

1. Gain strength in numbers and unity in purpose.

As God nudges, bring others into the team. Meet regularly to pray, learn, organize, and continually evaluate your blueprint for educating the congregation about making your church a place of welcome. A leader or coleaders should oversee the work of the entire team to advocate, model, and implement hospitality for and by the congregation.

2. Open each meeting with a direct focus on God.
    Read from the scriptures.

    > How lovely is your dwelling place, O Lord ... What joy for those who can live in your house, always singing your praises ... A single day in your courts is better than a thousand elsewhere. (Psalm 84:1, 4, 10a NLT)

    Share devotional writings, such as the following from Oswald Chambers.

    > The fountains from which love flows are in God, not in us. It is absurd to think that the love of God is naturally in our hearts, as a result of our own nature. His love is there only because it "has been poured out into our hearts by the Holy Spirit" (Romans 5:5).[6]

    Pray together.

    > Begin by sitting silently. *Imagine your church being all that God plans.* Ask for guidance. Listen. Prayer is enhanced when team members pray audibly. Invite "speaking" a word or phrase to invoke God's specific lead to do the following:

    - Gather more team members.
    - Help educate the congregation.
    - Create a welcome center.
    - Have God's love flow throughout our church.

3. Generate various ways to educate the congregation. Here are just a few:
    - Create hospitality reflections for the bulletin. (See Appendix 3.)
    - Have brief testimonials in worship of why individuals felt welcomed into the congregation.
    - Plan a "Hospitality Happening"—a friendship dinner, a historic English tea, a soup-and-salad social. Start with imaginative get-acquainted activities. Provide instrumental music and creative sing-along songs to suit the theme. Have hospitality humor—"doing it wrong but telling it right." Include scriptures, prayers, and the oral support of the pastor.
    Stop! Have you considered the scope of this project? Are you intending to educate a small portion of the congregation, a large portion, or what? You could follow the steps taken by our covenant group (mentioned earlier in the chapter), or you can

set your own course. Either way, let God be your guide. Remember the goal is to have everyone *enjoy* hospitality as they *learn* about it.

- "Inviting Sunday"—strongly promote and encourage congregational participation. Current attenders are urged to bring guests. As models, all members of designated sub-teams are expected to do so and sit with their guests. This helps assure there will be numerous guests. Another sub-team will set up and serve a simple meal of finger foods after each worship service. It is impossible to be a good host to someone and, at the same time, to be a valuable member of the food-serving sub-team: Both roles would suffer.

  Guests are the priority! Additionally, greeters and ushers should be prepared to provide loving outreach. With genuine hospitality flowing, guests, hopefully, will feel valued and gain a sense of connection—perhaps belonging.

4. Remain attentive to other creative ideas God puts in your heart and head.

    Be faithful. Imagine. Dream. Pray! God will continue to guide you and your congregation. Step up your purpose and passion. Step up your willingness to advocate, plan, dig in, and involve many others. Innovate. Hospitable congregations serve up a taste of home.

Step Up Your Ministries to Expand Hospitality

Outsiders and insiders, rejoice together! (Romans 15:10 MSG)

- Create a staffed welcome center.
  This space for grace is designed especially for newcomers, but it serves all who gather. Here, a friendly face, a watchful eye, and a kind "May I help you?" can send a message of invitation to receive literature and verbal information, to join us in worship, and to accept our love.
- Have a coffee area open after every service.
  This ministry is to be promoted as a place to meet and greet others, especially newcomers.
- Name tags are to be worn by the current church family, certainly those serving as greeters, ushers, and hosts.
  This offers an approachable appearance, but never ask a guest to wear a name tag.
- As newcomers enter or leave the sanctuary, present them with a small gift accompanied by a smile. Offering a gift to someone is a kind gesture of welcome. It also creates an opening for conversation and future relationships. The gift could include an attractive bag or mug

with "fillers," a brochure advocating opportunities to connect, a scriptural confirmation that God loves them.

- Keep watch on seats in the back, specifically for visitors.

  Visitors frequently come in late and slip out early. Without vigilance, they can be in and out without being made welcome. During worship, greeters and ushers should carefully monitor the congregation, focusing on the people sitting near the back. Greeters and ushers should discreetly attend to visitors' needs.

- Use attendance pads.

  Sign-in books gather information about members as well as guests. This enables a follow-up for both. Visitors appreciate an unexpected gift or note personally delivered or mailed to their homes. Members who have been absent for several weeks feel they are cared for when they receive a call of concern.

- Have a formal visitor welcome during worship.

  Extend a general welcome: "To all visiting today, we are grateful you chose to join us. When you are here, you are family. We hope you will return." Do not ask visitors to identify themselves by standing, raising their hands, or giving their name aloud. Statistics show that 66 percent of people are uncomfortable with such exposure. An exception may be in a tourist town in which people are passing through. Pastors, invited community leaders, and former members now living out of the area often appreciate a public introduction, but not the average church visitor.

- Include the words "visitors and guests" in a prayer during worship and classes.

  When we pray "for all visitors and guests with us today," we communicate our love for them. These folks get a glimpse of the power and purpose of prayer without being made to feel vulnerable.

- Create a "Get to Know You" plan to welcome visitors.

  Newer findings for the current culture indicate *the congregational greeting in worship is the most dreaded time for newcomers and the unchurched.* Forced introductions can feel awkward for many. In a church that uses the tradition of "passing the peace," the congregation should understand its meaning and intent. (See Appendix 4.) Welcomes are often more natural and more authentic when they occur one-on-one. Chris Walker, evangelism coach, recommends that the optimum time to connect with newcomers is *immediately following the service.* Trained hosts should make every effort to do just that.

After words of welcome, "meaningful small talk" should happen.[7] You can open with something like, "I don't believe we've met. My name is_____."

Here are some continuations:

"Do you live in the area?"
"It's been great to meet you and worship with you."
"Glad you came. I hope you will come again."
"I've been a member here for_____. The ministries and people are great."

Step Up Your Congregational Welcoming Practices

Welcome one another, therefore, just as Christ has welcomed you, for the glory of God. (Romans 15:7 NRSV)

In the monastery where the Benedictine monks lived was this early custom: when a guest comes, we welcome them as if they were Christ. To highlight this practice, at their doorway were these words: "Where hospitality is present, Christ is present." In our churches, we need reminders as well. Whether the stranger is like us or quite different, *we* are to welcome them as if they were Jesus himself.

All-Points Bulletin Made Known to Each Member

Everyone you encounter is on God's most-wanted list.

Hospitality is powerful; it touches something deep inside every person. All human beings have a basic need to belong. As a member of God's family, I am, simply put, to help others belong to God.

Roles for Every Member

1. I am God's representative.
2. I am to imitate God.
3. I am part of God's plan to welcome, invite, and bring others into God's house.

Members should learn to recognize a visitor. To discover newcomers, members must intentionally look for them.

New faces: Anyone you do not know may be a visitor or a member. If you don't know them, you should get to know them.

Insecure body language: People walking tentatively, changing directions, or projecting a questioning look need a friend—so go be one. A pleasant "Can I be helpful?" is a good start.

The thought of mistaking a member for a visitor—a member you have never met or have forgotten—can be intimidating. But never let that prevent you from reaching out to others. If you do make a mistake, keep it light; smile or laugh, as is appropriate. Ask forgiveness and express gladness that you have finally met—or *re-met*.

Every regular attender should make greeting visitors a priority. When newcomers are spied, *visitor advantage* applies: If they are not preoccupied, go to them before stopping to chat with those you already know. After warmly exchanging introductions, a nice upgrade to the welcome is asking permission to introduce them to others. Multiple introductions provide more opportunity to discover people with whom they have an affinity. If the newcomers accept your offer, be discerning: How many introductions are too many?

Step Up to God's Heart—Be All In

> And the Lord added to their numbers daily, those who were being saved. (Acts 2:47 NIV)

Relationships are a vital part of the Christian faith. We relate to visitors, aware they are children of God we may not yet know. In reaching out to them, we acknowledge and express their great worth to God, Father of us all. We invite them to be part of our household of faith so they can continue or begin a relationship with Jesus, who welcomes them in love as Savior and friend.

Our gracious welcome to visitors should clearly convey the love and esteem *we* place upon them as well; we partner with God. *Where hospitality is present, Christ is present*—even in our churches today. This gives us hope: insiders and outsiders might grow together in relationship with God the Father, Son, and Holy Spirit—that's everybody; that's all in.

Hospitality Challenge

1. Why is prayer so essential to developing God's hospitality? Share your thoughts.
2. Ponder the notion, "True hospitality runs through all that the church does." If this idea is part of your personal vision of God's hospitality, suggest ways the vision team, the trustees, and the staff can have positive effects on the hospitality mission of your church. Consolidate your suggestions with those of like-minded members. Then make an appointment with the church governing leadership so you can advocate for true hospitality throughout the church.
3. With permission granted to build a team, build—but start slowly.
    a. Review the ideas in this chapter, and note its appendices.
    b. Which images within the vision are doable, considering your human and material resources?
    c. Initially, the primary focus is to educate, train, and activate the team.
    d. As the team becomes established, emphasis must be given to enlighten, encourage, and enthuse others about extending hospitality to all.
    e. Seek God's help often, especially when implementing a new ministry.
    f. Creatively and consistently remind the congregation of biblical truths about hospitality.
    g. Keep the vision of a hospitable church before the congregation. Display short verbal images strategically throughout the church: "Open Hearts. Open Minds. Open Doors"; "Roles for Every Member" (included previously in this chapter); "God's Hospitality Experienced Here!"
    h. Invite others to join the team so they can help lead in growing God's hospitality. (See Appendix 5.)
4. For realistic scenarios that can be problematic yet hold promise, see Appendix 6.
5. Consider an all-church hospitality experience: Personally invite the entire congregation, heartily entreating them to come. It should be prescribed and presumed that all team members will attend.

A church in the grip of an ingrown culture might miss or ignore God's call to a heart for hospitality. Plan for the whole church to study and learn hospitality together. Find or create a series of lessons that is relevant and befitting for worship and for small groups of children, youth, and adults, as well as take-home ideas. (See Appendix 7.)

When hearts and minds are awakened and freed, better attitudes and behaviors may emerge. If so, your congregation will have become a touch more hospitable. *Keep on keeping on.*

Team Prayer

Sit quietly. Now take a minute to just imagine what God wants to do in your church and how God might choose to use you. Read the poem "Just Imagine" (included immediately following this chapter) slowly and prayerfully. Let's wait for God to speak on God's time. Amen.

Personal Prayer

Loving, welcoming God, I long to feel the drumbeat of your love in my heart. Give me a vision of your hospitality in my mind and for our church. Fill me, fill us, with your Holy Spirit to help make it happen. Amen.

Pray this prayer for thirty days. Practice receiving God's loving hospitality into your own life and then let it flow out into the lives of others.

JUST IMAGINE

You are by yourself, but not alone.
> Aware of a Presence,
> Surrounded by love
> Bigger, larger more enveloping than ever before.

Out of the quiet comes glowing glory.

Then, a whisper, *"You are mine… I love you… I am with you."*

You speak out loud,
> "I am loved, I am loved!"
> The thought comes: *I can risk loving others.*

Then People—many people, all kinds of people—walking through a church door.

"My church?" you ask.

They come, and keep coming.
> Many you know, and strangers,
> Some real surprises,
> Even offenders, some currently living in the shadow of evil.

Such a mixture of faces you have never seen all in one place.
> Children, youth, families, singles; strong and mature, feeble and broken.
>> A medley of races and nations, and yet…

There is connecting—with laughter, joy and jubilation; some tears, caring for one another.
> Visitors invited to belong, and strangers made welcome.
>> Recognition that all are children of the same Creator God.
>> Here in God's "dwelling place." No one is left out—no one.
> Yes, togetherness, like never before.
> It's euphoric. It's glorious. It's Divine!

There is learning, knowing and growing—all ages and stages.
There is praying, lots of praying: alone and in small groups, together as God's people.

There is worship, powerful and Spirit-filled worship:
        With quiet—calm and call.
        Praise and presence, Holy Presence,
        Holy and Hope-filled,
        Proclaiming God's Word.

And love—God's Spirit waving over *our* spirits—it's everywhere:
        The Transforming love of God in Christ Jesus!

Then there is the *cross*, the offering, the sacrifice.
        Forgiveness: new life for me, for you.
        Room at the foot off the cross for everyone,
        God's Ultimate Hospitality for all!

        Silence and surrender, surrender to God's will.

There is meeting and planning, advocating, cooperating, supporting…
        There is seeking God's provision; there is challenge to provide and protect.
        There is caring for needs: small needs, big needs—here, there and everywhere.
        There is self-sacrifice: feeding, making space, creating a family.
        A household of faith.
        There are "markers" to live by: loving God, loving neighbor.

        God casts the vision; the vision is caught—it keeps developing, creating.

There is going out…
        Reconciliation with family, coworkers and foes.
        Gleaning places, welcoming the poor.
        Projects for neighbor and community, release from trenches of hopelessness.
        Imitating God, as a Child of God;
        Becoming "Little Christs"…in an apathetic and broken world.
        Inviting others to come.

There is returning…

    Keeping Sabbath: Restoration, Renewal, Rest in the Lord.

It's *then* you hear the beat, *a soft recurring rhythmic beat…*

    A gentle drumbeat? A heartbeat?

    It's the Drumbeat of God's Heart, beating in love for every creature ever created—

    Even the vilest offender.

    The beat continues, and soon it begins to beat softly and quietly in *your* heart.

And then a vision of your church returns…

You sense the beating of God's heart in other hearts, in this House of God.

    One heart, another heart, and another…

    Beating in the House of Prayer for all people;

    The place you call "My Church—God's Church"

        The Beat of Love:

    God's Love: Father, Son and resurrected Spirit of Christ!

Beating in many, so more may know: "Come, *you* belong, God delights in you!"

The Beat goes on! It's happening!

God's hospitality is flowing throughout this church

And God smiles!

CHAPTER 8

Expectations of Hospitality Ministers: Equipping "Specialists"

Equip God's people to do his work and build up the church,
The body of Christ.
—Ephesians 4:12 (NLT)

As visitors in New York City on a Sunday morning, we entered a church. Standing by the door was a male greeter who welcomed us and informed us there was seating left only in the balcony. Immediately, a woman stepped forward and declared, "I will take care of them." She addressed us warmly, making us feel valued. Giving assurance we would be able to sit on the main floor, she intended to find us a place. It became clear this was her assigned task. "Please wait here. I will be right back." After a brief time, she returned and apologized. The seats thought to be available had been taken, but she would locate others.

Suddenly, a woman who had been seated came down the aisle and said to us, "Come with me. I have seats for you!" We followed to where she had been sitting. There, she gathered her coat, purse, and books and then offered, "I want you to sit in our seats." When we resisted a bit, she smiled and said, "No, please, it's my joy to share them with you." Then the first woman came by and made certain we were comfortably situated. She thanked the woman for sharing her space. We had never experienced such sacrificial hospitality in a church.

This is an excellent example of a *trained* hospitality minister and another caring member of the congregation teaming to connect with visitors. The usher found us, made us feel honored, and made it known that we needed seats. The *spontaneous* hospitality minister, sitting in the congregation waiting for her friend, gave us their seats.

The members of this congregation with whom we could pleasantly and gratefully interact illustrated important truths. For a church to really have a heart for bringing others into the kingdom of God, it must be deliberate about welcoming them into God's house and be properly prepared to do so. Then, it must make them want to return. All this necessitates having a core of people, each equipped to fulfill one or more very specific responsibilities. And whether or not persons in the congregation are *specialists*, there should be very many of them ready to spontaneously show love to anyone who enters.

Specialists set a tone, a foundation, and a standard for others to emulate, build upon, and improve. In one church, Erma, Mary, and Bill are prepared, passionate greeters. Their eyes, smiles, words, and touch spell out, "We are so glad you came." Joan and Sandy help at a community meal and worship service on a weekday. Along with greeting and welcoming, they key on connecting with others through conversation, fellowship, and serving them a hearty dinner.

Demeanor, knowledge, and flexibility are assets required of Linda, Nina, Tauna, and John as they minister to people throughout the week at the church's welcome center. Such trained ministers respond to folks who may need one or more of these: use of a restroom, a bag of groceries, a voucher for gasoline or lodging, someone to listen, someone to pray, or someone to say, convincingly, "God loves you!" At one Sunday service, Cindy roved among the congregation, ready to give a hug to any willing recipient. It represented her Christian love *and* God's love for that person. And she was convincing.

Dedicated Christians performing explicit tasks must be an integral part of any church hospitality pursuit. Many factors will contribute to the development of a comprehensive, customized plan that includes precise job descriptions and training procedures. Here is a start:

- building size and facilities
- active-membership data
- individual gifts and talents
- community characteristics
- financial resources
- the magnitude of a desire for reaching out to others

I am hopeful that the ideas, examples, and suggestions contained herein will be helpful in planning and providing hospitality by and through your church—helpful whether you have ten members or ten thousand members. May the Holy Spirit light the way.

Indoor Ministries

Greeters and Ushers and Hosts—Oh My!

The first impressions of a church that folks receive are bravely entrusted to these front-liners. Making people feel wanted, helping them connect with others, and planting a sense of belonging extend far beyond the duties traditionally assigned to greeters, ushers, and hosts.

- As the Spirit mandates disciples to overflow with love:
  - We greet people as if they were Jesus himself.
  - We usher people into the kingdom of God.
  - We host people who join us, hoping all will move closer to God.
  - We extend God's hospitality in the church, God's house, where all are welcome.

- We must intentionally offer much of ourselves as we offer God's hospitality:
  - We know hospitality with our *hearts*. To love the invisible God, we must love the visible neighbor.
  - We reflect hospitality with our *eyes*. Do not glance away; stay focused on our guests. Viewing people as "in the image of God" is very different.[1]
  - We utter hospitality with our *mouths*. Caring words, genuinely spoken, are very welcoming.
  - We bestow hospitality with our *hands*. A befitting touch initiates connecting.
  - We confirm hospitality with our *ears*. Listen intently to our company.
  - We think hospitality with our *heads*. Be mindful of doing small kindnesses.

- Deliberate ways to connect and minister with newcomers:
  - Open doors for them.
  - Approach people; walk to meet and greet them. Engage your *heart* first and then the rest of you.
  - Present your hand as you introduce yourself: "Welcome to_____Church. My name is_____."
  - Offer assistance to adults with children. Acknowledge the children and talk to them. Show the adults what is available (e.g., activity totes, children's bulletins, rocking chairs, etc.).
  Inform them of a nursery, but *never* insist they take the children from the sanctuary.
  - Introduce newcomers to others.
  - Walk with them to a restroom or other places in the church they wish to go.
  - Help people find seats close to friendly members.

- Gently offer instructions for using significant items (e.g., bulletins, attendance pads, hymnals, visitor cards, prayer cards, etc.).
- After worship, invite and take them to the welcome center or the refreshment area.
- If possible, introduce them to the pastor.
- Request contact information from new people so that someone can follow up.
- "Subtly collect contact information so that someone can follow up. Most newcomers, especially the unchurched, are reluctant to sign anything."

Pew Host or Spotter Ministry

Individuals who oversee a specific area in the worship setting are called pew hosts or spotters. Each one locates in an assigned area, intending to greet everyone there, connecting with as many as possible before the service begins. The radar of these ministers must be sharply attuned for identifying and responding to someone new.

Greeters, ushers, and spotters can be trained to perform each other's duties. Whenever those who are scheduled for an assignment cannot fulfill it, they are to find a replacement. Offering a welcome gift to a new person, helping people with children feel welcome (even if the children are restless and a bit noisy), and reacting readily and kindly to the many other occasions that may arise are part of the expectations for these specialists—and the reasons they serve.

Welcome Center and Refreshment Area Hosts

Every host at these busy traffic hubs must be gracious and accepting to all. They must treat folks with sincere love and respect, including those who hoard cookies, spill drinks, or leave trash. For people who speak, act, appear, or otherwise seem unwashed, EGR (extra grace required) must be fulfilled.

All these well-trained volunteers are afforded many opportunities to initiate influential connections that may lead to lasting relationships with a church family. Conversations with the guests should be as the writer of Ephesians teaches: "Do not let any unwholesome talk come out of your mouths, but only what is helpful for building others up, according to their needs, that you may benefit those who listen" (Ephesians 4:29 NIV). Additionally, it is important that these ministers be aware of happenings within the church and can answer relevant questions or find someone who can.

Every Christian should ask the question, "What can I do to build up others?" The following saying hangs in the room where I have morning devotions: "Share Faith—Offer Prayer—Gather Hope." Each of us should strive always to benefit people in our midst, making every effort to give them hope before they leave our presence.

Reinforce Connections by Reconnecting—Soon!

Reach out to newcomers within forty-eight hours after their church visitation. Evidence indicates this tends to produce good results. An earnest gesture of personal interest from a member or the pastor should convey, "We are very happy you came and hope you will return." This message of gladness and continuing invitation—presented with sensitivity—should encourage but not engage. It is meant to make a recent visitor feel wanted but not chased. Using this approach, the message and messenger are usually pleasantly received.

These follow-up messages can be delivered by phone, mail, or a doorstep visit. Small gifts, such as homemade bread, jelly, or a bag of popcorn, could be dropped off with a warm smile and a simple, creative note. There should be no intent to go inside the home, just a loving presence at the door. If no one answers, the gift should be left to be discovered.

Creative Note Ideas

- Jesus is the bread of life. Come again; experience more *life* with us.
- Pop in to join us another time soon!
- Come back to "taste and see that the Lord is good."

Let the Holy Spirit lead your note-writing creativity.

Hallway Hosts

For the safety and security of our children and youth and for the overall hospitality of the congregation, a cordial and welcoming person walking the halls can do much to express how we value all people. This should not be viewed as police monitoring but as an act of love.

On Christian holidays and on special Sundays when there may be more guests than usual for children's programs, musicals, honoring veterans, or celebrating a hallmark of the church, extra hosts are very often appreciated in the hallways to give a gracious smile, a cheerful greeting, and directions.

Outdoor Ministries

This is a true story of a small-town postmistress whose child had died. She was not connected with any church. One Sunday, several months after the death, some church members found her sitting in her car in the church parking lot, crying. They invited her to come inside with them. As she walked toward the church with her new friends, she said, "I have come here for six Sundays and did not have the courage to come inside." Yes, churches *do* need outside greeters.

Parking Lot Attendants

Having someone in the parking lot with an umbrella (if needed), a smile, and a gesture of where one might park is quite helpful. For those who have never been to church or are not church-friendly, this can be exactly the encouragement they need to enter an unfamiliar or uncomfortable environment. A walkie-talkie or cell phone connection between the attendant and the inside greeter enables sharing of information concerning the newcomers. The greeter can truthfully say, "You have been expected."

Valet Parking

Parking vehicles is a select but valuable ministry that can be offered. It is particularly helpful to older or disabled members, as well as guests. Valet parking is just one example of a loving church striving to satisfy a need, even if only a few have that need.

Job Descriptions, Training, and Schedules Are Necessary

Each church must decide to what extent they hope to be God's house, providing God's hospitality. Then vital assets need to be evaluated. I'm not referring to facilities and finances but to spiritual conviction, determined commitment, and the personal gifts and talents within the church.

In the body of Christ, each person has gifts and should be given opportunities to use them. Yet to be part of an efficient and effective hospitality team, those gifts must be developed and directed. Our study and worship remind us that spiritual conviction includes knowing that God has expectations of us. Extending hospitality well is one of them. Perhaps the hardest asset to measure and maintain is commitment. Without it, we can end up tapping unprepared people on Sunday morning, asking them to greet or usher. Not only does this disregard the importance of these roles, but it could distract from the peace and purpose of the worship service.

To help avoid such scenarios, the following are necessary and fundamental components of any hospitality plan:

- ❖ Educate the congregation about God's hospitality.
- ❖ Create detailed job descriptions, flexible enough to evolve.

❖ Devise training sessions that include best practices, after-action reports, and role-playing to enact what-ifs.

❖ Produce extensive assignment schedules with backup procedures.

❖ Encourage people to commit to a job and do it well.

Beyond Sunday Morning

More Hosts, Please

If your church has weekday activities such as daycare, nursery school, or after-school tutoring, you may want to consider a host at the entrance area during the busiest times. This is another way to connect with people who come into your church but do not attend worship on Sunday. Positive relationships can be established—and strengthened as you invite them to worship services. You should make these folks aware of relevant programs the church has to offer.

For funerals or community gatherings, as in voting locations, hosts may be highly regarded. Strategically stationed and wearing friendly faces, they can open doors, give directions, furnish an escort, and join in good conversations that edify the people and the occasion.

Are there outside groups that want to use the facility? Self-help groups, Scouts, music groups, and sports teams often need a place to gather. If a church member has an interest in some group members or activities, that person could be a good connector between life in the group and life in the church. For each group, someone should at least ask permission to visit their meetings and invite their members to programs and services.

Because of the vast number of people who have never been to a church or have not recently connected with one, it is crucial to extend hospitality beyond your walls. This is known as *contact ministries*.

Hospitality at Community Events

Whether it is a parade, festival, or another town observance, your church has an opening to be hospitable. Equipped with smiles and small gifts, even cups of cold water on a hot day, volunteers can present this care from your congregation. On a cold day, it's hot chocolate; near Christmas, candy canes.

During these celebrations, visual displays can highlight some of the ministries your church provides. Perhaps coming events can be promoted cleverly on a small handout that includes the church address and contact information. Also, having an easily identified box for prayer requests is very appropriate. For someone who seems desperate, there should be volunteers prepared to respond by listening to, praying with, or otherwise helping the person as needed. Contact ministries simply blend a presence of your church with the general public of your community. That presence is a subtle invitation to come and be with you in God's house.

But ... *what if they accept?*

Company's Coming!

You had better get ready.

Having the Church Say "Welcome," Outside and Inside

- *Grounds that are safe, convenient, and attractive*: Visitor and disabled parking should be near the main entrance. There must be disabled-accessible ramps and doors. Walkways are to be clear and safe. A children's outdoor play area must be safe and decorated appropriately. All areas should be beautified with shrubs, flowers, and well-manicured lawns. Consider having a large outdoor nativity for Christmas.
- *Outdoor lighting, signs, and entryways:* Day and night, the church needs to tell the public its name, worship times, and mission. Signs with sources of light should direct people to parking areas. Entrances are to have easily visible Enter signs. Also, signs at doors not intended as entrances should direct folks to the nearest entryway of the building.
- *Inside of entryways:* These thoroughfares ought to remain free of brooms, buckets, salt, shovels, repair tools, and other maintenance items. There should be adequate lighting; a dark entrance signals not to come in. A soft light from a table lamp suggests a warm, inviting aura. Flowers and other indoor plants brighten the soul.
- *Essential signs inside:* If you want to know how effective your direction and destination signs are, invite someone totally unfamiliar with your facility to walk through and discover all the locations where activities occur and signs are needed. The sanctuary, nursery, classrooms, offices, and restrooms must be clearly marked, as well as the arrows that point the way.
- *Five-star restrooms:* Clean, fragrant, child-friendly restrooms are an absolute must. A small basket containing complimentary sanitary products, emery boards, and Band-Aids will add a touch of home.
- *Uncluttered shelves and rooms:* Church rooms are used often by more than one group and for more than one purpose. Clutter left lying around is disrespectful of any intended worthwhile use of the room. It is inhospitable to those present and to those who will follow.
- *An indoor area for children that is clean, attractive, child-friendly, and safe:* Parents are sensitive to these requirements; they expect them for their children. Jesus was very clear: "Let the children come unto me." If you want children and their families to come and keep coming, you have to help them want that too.

- *A people-friendly church facility:* Maintaining the integrity of the structure and the proper functioning of the internal systems will preserve the comfort and well-being of members and visitors alike. Quality furnishings and aesthetic effects are inviting and welcoming to all. But if these niceties become budget-busters, they can be subsidized by the gifts and talents of the congregation. Trustees hold a great responsibility for the upkeep of the church. If hospitality is believed to be imperative, it *will* happen.

Hospitality Ministers and the Purpose of God

God plants the spirit of love in the hearts of people. If that love is not given careful attention, it remains alive but of little use to God's purpose. In the hearts of hospitality ministers, God's love should be cherished and cultivated. It is to grow, mature, and bear the fruit of the Spirit. The seeds of the fruit hold the identity of their Source, the very image of God, and a living and powerful purpose.

God's purpose is to have new seeds planted in the hearts of others. God calls upon hospitality ministers and all Christians to plant, nourish, and continue to care for these seedlings so others may know God and realize they have the spirit of love within them. Love from God is fully retained by each person, even as it flows through them and into another—a wonderful reason why hospitality ministers receive so much joy as they partner with God in planting new seeds.

Hospitality Challenge

You have seen a partial picture of what is required to provide God's hospitality to others.

1. Can a church offer active and effective hospitality amid torn tapestries, peeling paint, and faulty furnaces? Explain your answer.
2. Are your mind, heart, and spirit in agreement or conflict about the hospitality that God expects of you? Take time to consider all of what your answer means.
3. Assume that you have the spiritual conviction to be part of a hospitality team and the determined commitment to stick with it. Make a list of all your gifts and talents that can be used on the team for God's purposes.
4. Complete the hospitality evaluation. (See Appendix 2.) Where do you rank your church? Compare and discuss your ranking with those of others who have completed the evaluation. How might the cumulative results of all such evaluations be used to improve hospitality in your church?
5. Complete the hospitality audit. (See Appendix 8.) Give a copy of the composite audit to your trustees and to the members of the governing body.

Prayer

Radiating Christ

Dear Jesus,
Help us to spread Your fragrance everywhere we go.
Flood our souls with Your Spirit and life.
Penetrate and possess our whole being, so utterly,
    that our lives may only be a radiance of Yours.
Shine through us, and be so in us,
    that every soul we come in contact with
    may feel Your presence in our soul.
Let them look up and see no longer us,
    but only Jesus.
Stay with us, and then we shall begin to shine
    as You shine;
So to shine as to be a light to others.
The light, O Jesus, will be all from You,
    none of it will be ours;
It will be You shining on others through us,
Let us thus praise you in the way you love best
    by shining on those around us.
Let us preach you without preaching,
    not by words but by example,
By the catching force, the sympathetic influence
    of what we do,
the evident fullness of the love our hearts beat to
You. Amen

—John Henry Cardinal Newman[2]

PART IV

How Are We to Live Out God's Hospitality?

Imitating Christ Will Be Our Challenge;
the Spirit Will Be Our Power

CHAPTER 9

God's Invitation Is to All: So We Are to Invite

When they said, "Let's go to the house of GOD," my heart leaped for joy.
—Psalm 122:1a (MSG)

"Emma, come," I hollered across the backyard. Emma is our son's family golden retriever. Her home is with us while our grandson receives treatment for a serious illness. Sometimes Emma comes immediately, but frequently she wants to do her own thing. So we must go after her. Usually, when we coax her, she is happy to come into the house.

Considering that 80 percent of the people in the United States have no meaningful connection with a church, it is obvious they need someone to go after them. They need to be invited home. Initially, our invitations may not be met by the psalmist's response: "I was glad when they said to me, 'Let us go to the house of the Lord'" (Psalm 122:1 NLT). We, however, should not be discouraged. The 80 percent do not yet realize the need to be changed and the wealth that awaits. God's hope for every person is to have an abundant life in the kingdom and to become a full member of God's family. For those of us already in the family, God calls us to go after others—befriend, invite, and encourage them—*to come home.*

Why We Must Pursue Them

I have studied and applied church hospitality for over two decades, and I am convinced of some reasons why people do not find their way home through our churches.

93

➢ *Church has not been a significant part of their background.* People who have never or rarely attended a church or those who have been absent for a long time may not have church on their radar. Some may have negative views of the institutional church. (See Appendix 9.) These people simply do not envision themselves in a church. Being unaware of the love and joy that believers can offer them or having witnessed tainted versions instead, why would they want to come?

➢ *Even people who consider church may feel very insecure about attending.* They don't know what to expect or how *to do* church. Reluctance and fear can surface, despite the Spirit nudging them to attend. They feel the divide and do not want to face rejection, so they mull questions like these:

- What will I find behind those doors?
- How should I act?
- Will I be included?
- Will I be judged for my habits or lifestyle?
- Will someone invade my space and hound me to return?
- Will they want money that I don't have?
- I've been to church before, and they hurt me. How can I trust them?

  After pondering such thoughts, people often don't take the risk.

➢ *Some do not come because they are not* personally *invited.* Studies show that from 70 to 90 percent of all the people who begin to attend a church were personally invited and brought to the church. Coming to a household of faith without a personal invitation or previous connection is not the norm. Folks not familiar with church, some who are hurting, those caught in the clutches of sinful behavior, introverts, and, in fact, most people need friendship and encouragement to enter the world of church.

Our culture often does not perceive and project church as the place to be. Caring friendships can help change that. When an individual comes with a friend who is a member of the church, they come with a built-in connection. Going to church feels less of a risk. But one friendly church member does not make an inviting church. Sad but true, people different from us might not be considered candidates for our congregations, either by us or them. Many unfriendly churches are dwindling, even dying.

A basic human need is *to belong.* Good restaurants couple satisfying this need with satisfying hunger. They pull out the stops to welcome an eclectic sampling of people and make them feel like family. How much more should we in the church embrace the truth that all people have a need and a hunger for God, which they might not yet recognize? God yearns for all to be satisfied. God's plan is that we bring others into the family and help them receive the nourishment they have been missing.

People Need Coaxing Too

If we take our eyes off Emma dog, we may not see her wander from the house and into trouble. People, left to their human bent, tend to wander away from God and God's house, not knowing the huge trouble that brings. We must intentionally and consistently coax them to come. Otherwise, they will miss the endless benefits of dwelling in the presence of the God who loves them and wants them as full members of the family. Christians are to represent Jesus, our gracious Host. We, his church, are charged with the task of extending his invitation to all. We are to host others in Jesus' name.

Here is a story of a couple who needed to be coaxed:

Emily and Stan are wonderful people, well loved and respected in the community. Church was not part of their present lifestyle. But Emily's beloved Christian mother lived with them, and they deeply admired her faith. They poured themselves into bringing joy to her life. When she died, they were grief-stricken. As I spent much time with them, planning the funeral, I learned of still more pain in their lives. Broken relationships with their children were causing them anguish. Meanwhile, I sensed God prodding them to return to church.

How could I be invitational in a way that would show promise, since they had been unchurched for so long? I prayed ... stalled ... prayed ... stalled.

Finally, I invited them to church, saying, "We will sit with you in the pew where your parents sat for many years."

Emily replied, "Thank you so much for your kind invitation. This is just the nudge we've needed." Regular attendance is now part of their life.

Our friendship and their new relationships are growing. Best of all, they are experiencing the love of God, who is with them in their pain and in their joy. The church family to which they now belong is helping to heal the hurt of family losses they have endured. They thank me again and again for inviting them and connecting them with their new family—God's family.

Not all stories of *inviting* end this well. But for those that do, the kingdom of God grows, heaven rejoices, and we are inspired to do much more as invitational Christians.

A Firm yet Gentle Persuasion

The moral of Emily and Stan's story is this: Listen, love, pray, invite. Scripture is clear that *the Lord has given us the responsibility of persuading others* to come and be part of God's family. We can and we must do better than we are. The greatest impact we can make, even though it is uncomfortable in our culture, is to personally invite with bold intention. We can befriend and bring people to our churches. Real evangelism consists of genuine love and care, offering friendship and a continual invitation to experience God's love with and through our church families.

A comment Christians often make is, "I don't know who I would invite. All my friends are

Christians." That's a valuable observation—it clarifies the problem. If we Christians are to have a positive influence upon the world, infuse it with the love of Christ, and make disciples for its transformation, we must change our outlooks and increase our territory. We have to reach out with friendship evangelism. We must seek and welcome all who are not in God's family, including those unlike ourselves and those we don't yet call friends.

The "E-word"—evangelism—has become unfriendly and suspect at times because it has often been abused by confrontational methods. None of us should want to be a street-corner, horn-blowing, abrasive Christian. Nor should we choose to do anything like grabbing someone by the shirt and presenting in-your-face documentation, even if it is truth. Such behavior can make truth sound unbelievable and, at the very most, uninviting. Instead, we should pray for guidance and determination to speak with love, to listen with love, and to invite others to come and learn of God's love for them.

Everyone Is Invited? Really?

Yes! From the beginning of creation, God's invitation has been for all. This was profoundly reaffirmed by the report of Jesus' birth.

> The angel said, "Don't be afraid. I'm here to announce a great and joyful event that is meant for everybody, worldwide … *a Savior has been born for all people.*" (Luke 2:10–11a MSG; emphasis added)

Evangelism means "angel declaring." With our love in action, we must be *angels* on earth, declaring that the Savior is indeed for everyone. Unfortunately, much done in the name of evangelism has been anything but angelic declaration of good news for all people. If *how* we proclaim contradicts the truth of *what* we proclaim, people will not attend our churches. Overzealous love loses its scent and appeal; compassionate love retains the aroma of Christ and its attraction for all his beloved children.

Individual Christians, "Christ-ones," and the church collectively are to do the work of Jesus. As one man so appropriately stated, "The 20 percent who have a meaningful relationship with a church must assume the responsibility for helping the 80 percent who have no meaningful connection with a body of believers." Our assignment requires us to understand the full intent of Jesus' invitation. Each and every person is to know that Jesus wants them. All means all!

We should not become frustrated with those who have stopped attending our churches or those who seem to have had no interest in church. Rather, we should incur the longing of God's heart for these folks and relate to them graciously. Our words and ways cannot be judgmental. We have been equipped with good news that offers salvation to all people; we must share it lovingly and generously.

It is my deep conviction that any good transformation of the world will be slight at best until we Christians move out of our comfort zones and into true, active love. We are to help harvest many for the body of Christ. Planting seeds can begin in a workplace, school, neighborhood, gym, or sporting event. One-on-one connections and conversations can, over time, grow into friendships and invitations to join us in church. Our willingness to invite and bring others into a house of God must be resolute.

Once people attend our churches, there should be whole groups of church friends ready to support and inspire them on their journeys. We can also introduce them to specific persons who would help them develop and increase their faith. As the Spirit moves, the transforming love of Christ can make them become new disciples. New disciples are very contagious. They invite and bring others to come meet their church friends and see this Jesus they have met.

Blunders, Bloopers, and Blessings

Stories of my own inviting experiences include mistakes, rejections, and disappointments. But I believe we obey God when we invite others and trust to God that they will come. I have known the Spirit to take my weakness and present it as strength. We have been assured that every act of love we render under God's direction will bring fruit, whether or not we get to taste it.

Story 1

During a pre-marital counseling session with an unchurched couple living in a different town, I kept reminding them of their need for a church family. Because they lived some distance from my church, I continued to suggest churches in their area. The woman, Ashley, finally said to me, "Can't we come to your church?"

"Of course you can. We would love to have you. I just didn't think you would want to travel that distance," I admitted.

After the wedding day and with some encouragement, Ashley and her beautiful, outgoing daughter began attending. Then Ashley's husband came and occasionally grandparents and a great-grandmother. Eagerly, they became involved in ministries of the church. At a children's event, within Ashley's hearing, I said, "I just love to watch Ashley help. And to think I almost messed it up. She had to ask me, 'Can't we come to your church?'"

Upon hearing that, Ashley loudly called out, "And I am so glad we came here!"

The whole family had come home.

Story 2

Amber, a mother of four, exhibited responsible behavior against very tough odds. Still, she needed lots of resources and reassurance. Although mostly unchurched, she spoke of having attended a church as a child with her sister. I invited her and the children many times to come and connect. When I could not be available to meet her, I would plan for someone else to do so. But she wouldn't show. I was very disappointed. Finally, they began to attend weeknight ministries and some Sunday mornings. Frequently, the father would bring the children.

Amber began helping with our weekday ministries. We had much time to talk and share. She appreciated when I prayed with her. One day she told me of a great experience she had while cleaning the house. As she broke out singing "Jesus Loves Me," she was enveloped in a love she had never felt before. When I offered the invitation to be baptized, she accepted.

We continued to pray about her struggles. She said of the church, "I just feel like part of the family here."

Despite my blunders and disappointments, God used my obedience and blessed the work. Lives were lovingly touched, and there were more people in God's house. The Master so strongly states, "I want my house full!" (Luke 14:23 MSG).

Churches, Large and Small, Are to Advance God's Kingdom

It is noteworthy that any size church can be faithful and rewarded if it has an inviting spirit. Congregations continually look for low-budget ministries with high yield. Inviting and bringing others has the greatest potential for increasing our church families and advancing the kingdom of God. The initial expense is gumption and love.

As Christians, we embrace the prayer that Jesus taught his disciples. Most congregations pray regularly the powerful words, "Thy kingdom come, thy will be done." The intimacy of prayer draws us near to God, and God near to us. In that closeness, we open ourselves to God's heart and will. When we pray the Lord's Prayer fervently, we agree to take part in God's plan to expand the kingdom. The most straightforward way of doing so is to have an *intentional* invitational vision and mission as a pertinent part in the life of the congregation.

Often churches find it difficult to keep God's directive to invite. Far too often, I have heard Christians say, "God will send us the people who are to be here." The quote of a Lutheran pastor underscores our discomforts and rationalizations: "Once in every twenty-seven years, a Lutheran will invite someone to church." Church growth statistics confirm this is not far from reality in many established churches and denominations. We do not want to downplay God's direct work in the lives of people—inviting them to come home. Yet scripture clearly asserts that *God is making an appeal through us.* Relatively new and start-up churches grow as they spiritually invest in kingdom building and, one by one, invite and bring a friend, relative, associate, or neighbor to a church service or event.

But for too many churches, it remains unappealing to develop friendships for the sake of the kingdom. Being invitational while changing schedules and procedures to include new people may just seem too arduous. Unfortunately, there are those who are convinced that God doesn't want any more people in their congregation. Seriously? We must open our eyes to the light of truth that Jesus does invite all. We must listen to the words of Paul for the church at Corinth: "Because we understand our fearful responsibility to the Lord, we work hard to persuade others" (2 Corinthians 5:11 NLT). In our hearts, we know God's will!

Inviting others to church can cross personal boundaries for privacy. Becoming a friend of someone whose background we know only little about can intimidate. We don't want to infringe upon their space, and we don't want them to garner too much about ours. After all, faith is to be private—so says the world. Fear of entering another's territory, especially their faith, is often debilitating. However, the Bible fortifies us against such fear. Armed with faith and trust in Jesus, armed with God's love and our love for God, and armed with the power of the Holy Spirit, we are able to beat down fear and focus on our work—God's work.

We have been appointed to love, to share our faith, and to go make disciples. We can step into the task by extending invitations to come and connect with us. God's truth and instruction have given us hope and purpose for life. We should be excited to share that truth and instruction with others. When they respond to the love of Christ by believing in him and loving him in return, their hope and purpose will follow. And the kingdom of God will have grown.

Help Your Congregation Be Intentionally Invitational
Have a Plan

Start by designating a month or season, such as Advent or Lent, in which to emphasize inviting. This will give your congregation an opportunity to warm up to the prospect of inviting others. Then find innovative ways to implement the following ideas and procedures.

Steps to Becoming Invitational

1. Pray for the conviction to invite others.
2. Pray about whom to invite and how.
3. Invite your friend, relative, associate, or neighbor to something specific: worship service, Sunday school class, special program.
4. Bring your guest, sit with them, help them learn their way around, and introduce them to others.
5. When you have a guest, and church responsibilities prohibit you from staying with them, ask a church friend to partner with you by connecting with your guest.
6. Be alert to current attendees missing for an unexpected reason or an extended period. "We miss you" is usually appreciated.

7. Do not *badger*, but be consistent in love. Repeat your invitation. Be persistent but patient.

8. Pray, pray, pray for all persons involved with the plan or its activation, so God's hospitality happens!

Newcomers Need Care Similar to Newborns

The dubious news is that newcomers change our congregations; the good news is they bring new life! Assuredly, God has said, "I am about to do a new thing ... do you not perceive it?" (Isaiah 43:19 NRSV). When a newborn comes home, we hope there is a sense of welcome, a plan for inclusion, the intent to nurture, and the constant love and care that leads to growth, maturity, and continual assimilation into the life of the family. Should it be any different when a newcomer to our church home appears among our church family? We hope not.

Yes, for the *families*, a newborn and a newcomer do bring changes and challenges. But when they are received with love and dedication, there are high hopes and much joy for the new life and new opportunities. When growth is observed, there is reason to celebrate. It is also a time for reflection, rededication, and even revision to support continued growth. A strong foundation is still just a foundation.

Come

Congregations that seize the discipline of inviting others tend to grow in size and the will to follow God. They unite with God in building the kingdom. Building is maximized when many members have inviting frames of mind and heart. Being a thriving congregation aligned with God's love and desires for people is unbreakably linked to inviting those on the outside. But many of our churches fail to see the compelling connection. Pastors of some mega-churches have challenged their congregations to join God in changing this trend.

Andy Stanley promotes the challenge to be as easy as saying "Come and see!"[1] As for the thousands to whom he preaches, many invite and bring others. To Adam Hamilton, reaching beyond the walls of our churches to seek those who have lost their way is vitally important for faithful Christians. He urges diligence about imitating Jesus: "If this was Jesus' driving passion, it must be our driving passion in our churches."[2] So like Jesus, we are to take on not only words but a life-living, life-giving essence that says, "Come ... be with us as we grow in knowledge of God together."

However, healthy growth requires strong roots and plenty of nutrition. We break ground by changing a newcomer into "Ima Comer" or "Will B. Coming." Don't let these folks come in the front door and out the back before they have been warmly welcomed and shown a glimpse of Jesus through our eyes, touch, and words. For those who come, we can prayerfully and purposefully love them. We can help them become well-grounded and nourished by our Christian family and its scriptural beliefs. As they grow in the Spirit, each "Ima" and "Will" may be led to commit or recommit their lives to Christ. They would be connected to us and belong to God. Then we could all rejoice and sing, "I am so glad I'm part of the family of God." Perhaps another verse would be good: "I am so glad *you're* part of the family of God." Let's begin to invite!

Hospitality Challenge

1. Read the following scriptures, keeping in mind two questions:
   a. What is God saying to you?
   b. What is God saying to the church?

   - A song sung as people were going to the temple (Psalm 122:1).
   - An angel declared for whom Jesus came (Luke 2:10).
   - A story Jesus told as a reminder of God's intention:
   - "I want my house full!" (Luke 14:12–23).
   - Lost is being without the gift of salvation. Jesus saves people from themselves (Luke 19:1–10).
   - Paul instructed the church at Corinth about their responsibility to persuade others. How many times are the words *we, us,* and *our* used? (2 Corinthians 5:11, 14–21).

2. With God's directive and blessing before us, the biggest mistake we can make when it pertains to inviting others is to *not* invite them. How might God be leading you to help your congregation develop an intentional focus on inviting others? Share your thoughts with those who may have similar ones.

3. Let's have some *nuf*—I mean fun! Unscramble each group of letters below to disclose what we should do for all people inside and outside of our churches. If you need help, refer to the first paragraph of "Newcomers Need Care Similar to Newborns."
   ELVO ACER EMOCLEW RUNTRUE ICELUND

4. Why is the following sentence *not* redundant?
   "The intimacy of prayer draws us near to God, and God near to us."

Prayer

Lord of all life, thank you for inviting me to an abundant life. Remind me often that your ministry has always been to exhort others to come. Keep me humble; keep me loving. Help me and our congregation develop an invitational spirit so your house will be full. Amen.

CHAPTER 10

Sharing Our Faith with a World That Needs Good News

How can people have faith in the Lord and ask him to save them, if they have
never heard about him? And how can they hear, unless someone tells them?
And how can anyone tell them without being sent by the Lord?
—Romans 10:14–15 (CEV)

Picture this: "A sight to take your breath away. Grand processions of people telling all the good things of God" (Romans 10:15 MSG). Just imagine lots of people from every Christian church stepping out to share good news—the amazing things God is doing in their lives.

To many people in the world, such images would have little or no meaning. Some people deny God altogether, while many others are doubtful because they are not consciously mindful of God's great love for them and his presence in their lives. These folks may not know that God offers fresh starts and full forgiveness through the transforming love of Jesus. People can only put faith in the Lord and begin their salvation journey when they have heard about him. "And how can they hear, unless someone tells them?"[1] They can't! So who does God want to be the *someone*?

Christmas Connections

As I wrote this chapter during Advent, a recent event flooded my mind. On the square of the downtown area was a Hallmark scene: lights glowing, bows blowing, warmly clad people pressing against the chill of the evening, and the harmonic sounds and spirit of Christmas filling the air. This was the annual Cocoa Crawl, sponsored by the Downtown Business Council.

Christians from churches representing many traditions, along with other nonprofit organizations, had gathered together as a united presence to support and celebrate with the community. Each nonprofit team was assigned an area or station from which to give away smiles, good wishes, and their brand of cocoa. Our recipe? Mexican Hot Chocolate. Purposely requested, we were located right next to the manger display at the most centralized church in town. Here, folks were reminded that *God is present* among the people.

They streamed up and down Main Street and flowed in and out of shops, often with cocoa in hand. Many passers-by accepted song sheets and engaged in the joyous melodies of the evening. At one station, carols of the Christ child were sung, announcing the reason for the season and providing a most natural opportunity to share our faith. Some folks were content to sing or just listen to the music. Others desired to connect in conversation, including those who needed emotional or spiritual support.

The church was open for prayer in its candlelit sanctuary. Staff members were available for those who wanted someone to pray with them. Positioned outside were people sensitive and responsive to the needs of others. A welcoming gracious person, posted at a collection box, invited folks to leave prayer requests. Each request form asked, "Would you like a contact?"

From the prayer box came approximately fourteen requests, ranging from the loss of a child's kitten to the grief of two men who had lost their wives, their children's mothers. One request came from a student of the local college who was struggling with heavy personal concerns, including losses in her family back home. After the event, an alumna of the college was given the student's contact information. To her joy, she discovered she already knew the young woman. A call, a meeting for a milkshake, and an invitation to connect with a supportive church family allowed the incredible hope of Christ to be shared.

Consider Your Faith Journey

Who shared the good things of God with you—their lives, their love, their faith? Did someone challenge you to make a commitment to Christ? Continuing, if you will, what motivated you to become a Christian? Thinking back, what was foremost in your mind when you decided to follow Christ? Was it your need for salvation? Were you seeking a sense of peace? Perhaps you were prompted by the idea that God could help you get your life in order. Whatever your reason, you probably didn't become a Christian so you could tell other people about Jesus, did you? In fact, I suspect that becoming a salesperson for Christianity was just about the last thing on your mind.

Yet as we study the scriptures, one thing should be clear: when we become believers, our belief becomes alive only when we follow Jesus. Andy Stanley believes of all the challenges Jesus made of his followers, calling them to become "fishers of people" was at the top of the list. Regardless of your initial motives for receiving Christ, that's what Jesus wants for you as well—to help bring others to him.[2]

Rowing against the Current

The musical *Oklahoma* gave us the song "Doin' What Comes Naturally." For most of us, talking about our faith with others, especially those who do not believe as we do, doesn't exactly come naturally. Such encounters can be difficult and very uncomfortable, as is paddling upstream. But we are to obey Jesus' teaching. With resolve, follow his lead; with humility, forward his love; and with patience, fish—so his Father's house will be full. Sometimes the best fishing is upstream!

Jesus—the "Master Fisherman"

Jesus wants to *catch* every man, woman, and child. Some of his favorite lures are caring friendships, love, and forgiveness. People who are hungry for these and believe they are *real* latch on and are drawn into a relationship with him. Those who don't believe their validity or who hunger for other things instead search elsewhere. They will find an insatiable emptiness.

But we are fortunate. There were people who spent time with us in caring, loving relationships and told us about Jesus along our faith journeys. They were his apprentices. Now Jesus wants *us* to take up the trade. The great commission to "go therefore and make disciples of all nations" is not intended as an option (Matthew 28:19 RSV). Yet we resist doing it, and most of us don't do it very well. A sobering analysis of us as Christians was made by Mahatma Gandhi, a twentieth-century humanitarian and political legend, who said, "I like your Christ. I do not like your Christians."[3]

When Dr. E. Stanley Jones, missionary to India, asked Gandhi how we Christians can make Christianity more naturalized in India, not a foreign thing but a part of the natural life of India and contributing power to India's uplift, Gandhi is said to have replied without hesitation:

❖ First, I would suggest all of you Christians, missionaries and all, must begin to live more like Jesus Christ.

❖ Second, practice your religion without adulterating it or toning it down.

❖ Third, emphasize love and make it your working force, for love is central in Christianity.

❖ Fourth, study the non-Christian religions more sympathetically to find the good that is within them, in order to have a more sympathetic approach to the people.[4]

So how can Gandhi's profound critique of Christians, along with his suggestions, help us to catch fish for the kingdom—in our neighborhoods, in our spheres of influence, in the world? As Christians, we are called to follow and live like the most humble, self-sacrificing Jesus. We are expected to form relationships that, over time, will be tempered in trust, not toning down what we believe but exercising love so it becomes our strongest force and seeks the good in others. Then we can build on common ground. Gandhi, a Hindu, simply reminds us Christians to *do* what we have been taught. It begins with a heart willing to love and continues with an urgency to "follow the Fisherman."

Once our friendship, care, and love for another are felt as true, faith sharing becomes much more natural. Both the one who shares and the one who receives discover a deeper relationship with almighty God. So let's live out the commission we've been given, and do what we say we believe. Let's fish the way our Master teaches us.

While on earth, Jesus was a witness for his Father God. Jesus described God as powerful and creative, just and merciful, demanding and forgiving. Most important, Jesus taught how these characteristics were expressions of the Father's great, great love for every person. And just as Jesus shared this message of love from God, we are to live and share the message of love from Jesus. We are to be *his* witnesses. He equips us and is with us. But how should we begin?

Turn on Your Faith *GPS*

*G*enuinely Relate

Telling someone about Jesus and his love is good. Starting a new relationship by doing so often is not. People aren't likely to care about and be ready to receive what you know of God's love until they know how much you sincerely love and care for them. And that takes well-spent time together, earning their trust.

Lead by listening. Listen to their stories before presenting yours. How do they feel about their lives and the world around them? What changes are they hoping for? Learn where they are, in many respects, before trying to take them elsewhere. Failing to use this approach has led to abuse in the act of witnessing, harming both giver and receiver. Remember, Jesus is our model. He doesn't force himself upon people; acceptance would lose its meaning. We should not try to force Jesus upon anyone either. Offering and accepting Jesus and his love are heart things; they require a kinder, gentler manner. And the meaning of acceptance is life eternal with God!

While you listen to a person's story, listen for God to guide your responses. If their story includes a reference to God, wonderful—a door has been opened. Keep listening. If God is not mentioned, but their dialogue and demeanor imply a want or need for something more, a different door has been opened. Keep loving and continue to earn their trust with your genuine attention, interest, and empathy. Be expectant that God will tell you when to enter into *your* story and introduce God by name.

When you get your cue, share what you have seen, heard, and experienced that point to God. Emphasize the good things that God has done and is doing in your life. Then help the person recognize similar events in his or her life when God was present and provided something good.

Part of your story will likely include "God sightings" or "God moments." These are occasions in which we sense, physically or spiritually, the presence and power of God at work or the evidence of work completed. Such experiences can be big or small, subtle or stunning, but they are always laced with the beauty of God's love for us. They inspire and embolden us to share them with others, often spontaneously in small-group settings or one-on-one with other believers—*and with those who do not yet believe.*

Children in a Vacation Bible School were encouraged to share their God sightings. Some sensed God in a beautiful flower, a few when they watched a spectacular waterfall, and others while with family and friends. Some felt God when comforted after being hurt; some when they received an unexpected gift. Children often "see" more of God's handiwork than many of us. It's not because they look in the right places at the right times; creation and events are covered in God's fingerprints. God longs for us to slow down, eliminate some distractions, and be more observant. It will make us better witnesses, helping others to see too.

In the *Purpose-Driven Life* series, we are told that one of the five great purposes of our lives is telling others about Christ. We aren't told that it will be easy. Our comfort level will likely be tested. But remember, while people may not embrace our beliefs, they can never refute our experiences with God. If you are not taken seriously or are rejected, do not become defensive or choose to retreat. In such times, reflect on God's sovereignty, and negative feelings will dissipate.[5] Remain steadfast and allow God's love to continue through you and into those who hear.

Lock the following uplifting, faith-filled thoughts in your heart and mind:

Witnessing, according to John Fischer of the Purpose-Driven staff, is being so in love with God that you eventually end up talking about him. Witnessing is being so overwhelmed by the undeserved nature of your salvation that you can't contain your joy. Witnessing isn't coercing someone; it's quite the opposite. It's having someone coerce the gospel out of you because they can't stand not knowing what's going on with you anymore.[6]

*P*ray—Don't Start without It

Prayer is absolutely vital! It is how we communicate with God. Such communication requires getting very close, as in clinging to God for guidance, creating an intimate relationship of love and trust.

Prayer is necessary for ourselves and for those with whom we will share our faith. The more we are quiet and listen to God, the closer we will grow to him, and the more we will love him. And the more we love God, the more God's love will start to flow through us.[7]

TALKING to God is the first of two forms of prayer. It includes praise and gratitude and, as Jesus taught, *asking* for what we and others need.

- As we consider sharing our faith, we should pray that thoughts of inadequacy and other fears we may have are replaced with feelings of being empowered by the Spirit of God.
- For unique human relationships, ask God to strengthen the friendship and direct it toward the doors through which Jesus' love can be received.
- Once the doors to our friends' hearts have been opened, we must help our friends understand that *our* love for them streams beside the love *Jesus* has for them.

LISTENING to God is every bit as significant but seems more difficult. Saint John Vianney called it *mental prayer,* suggesting that to hear God, you should "shut your eyes, shut your mouth, and open your heart."[8]

- Prayer is where we are filled to overflowing, where "in the stillness of God" we are equipped with thoughts, words, and gestures that will come to us naturally at just the right time—keys to unlock doors.

In studying Mother Teresa's prayer life and her teachings, praying brings peace, unity, and joy into our souls and stirs up love that overflows to others. As our prayer lives grow, we discover our human nature alone is incapable of feeling peace, creating unity, sensing joy, and giving love as God gives. As to loving as Jesus commanded, especially those who are different or difficult, without praying, love does not happen.[9]

So let us pray!

Sharing Our Faith Stories

A Threefold Sketch of My Faith Story

Part 1: I was born into a loving family of faith. As a child, I attended Christian Endeavor, where I felt loved by people other than family. There, I learned to pray to a God of love, realizing Jesus was my friend. I could talk to him about anything. During my childhood faith-forming years, what I learned from Christian Endeavor complemented what I was taught at home.

Part 2: Around a campfire at church camp in my teen years, I responded to God's call on my life. On several occasions, I *dedicated* and *rededicated* my life to following Jesus, something I continue to do. On one occasion, I felt a call to full-time Christian service. Also during my adolescence, a friend died suddenly of acute leukemia. In my confusion, fear, and struggle, my associate pastor gently helped me to trust my life to Jesus and the hope he gives—in life and death.

Part 3: As a young adult on this part of my faith journey, I followed God's lead in seeking what the campfire call meant—attending college, embracing marriage, discovering the joys and challenges of parenting, and contemplating opportunities for ministry. It was a day-to-day faith walk for me. Then, the door opened for becoming an ordained deacon. That was the full-time Christian service to which I had been called as a young girl. It was incredible.

That tells you some of the highlights of *my* faith story. So that I am always ready to share it with others, I have committed it to mind, heart, and "wallet." That's right … I folded a three-by-five card horizontally into three equal sections. On each section, I put just enough words or simple drawings to depict one of the parts of my story. I then refolded the card and placed it in my wallet, so where I go it goes. Truth be told, I may forget my wallet, but I won't forget my story. (See Hospitality Challenge No. 1.)

Maintain Authentic Relationships

Building authentic relationships is not easy. Small acts of love are the key component in developing trust that creates human connections. Perhaps we should reread "Radiating Christ." (See chapter 8.)

In car races, a yellow flag means caution. In faith sharing, there can be numerous yellow flags. Proceed with confidence, but drive with caution. Do not come off the starting line as one who has it all together. Be ready and willing to set out with humility; then push forward with faith. No one has all the answers to living a Christian life. All of us struggle and have doubts from time to time. It is imperative to be authentic. We proclaim God has it all together, and we don't. That is exactly why we need a personal relationship with Jesus, our Savior, who knows the rough spots we may encounter. He walked this earthly walk. When asked how I am, an answer I have given is, "I'm okay; God is good!"

We should never dump the whole load of our burdens on those to whom we witness. But they do need to know we carry a load and have a God who wants to help. When the weight seems unbearable, we can cry out to God in our distress, as the psalmist did. God will hear, understand, and be pleased we have come to him—even when we ask why. And in God's wisdom and time, he will shoulder the portion of our load that is sufficient for us to continue.

Being open and honest about our struggles and doubts gives us opportunities to speak to what we discover about God during our turmoil. We are able to share the assurance that God hears us when we pray. We can testify to the times that God has been very near to us, especially when we were hurting. We can speak to the promise that God will never, ever leave us or forsake us.[10] At times, we might feel abandoned; we're not. God is the companion of our souls. When God has seemed far away, who do we think moved? And yes, there are those times when God, through his mighty power at work within us, has done more than we might ask or even imagine.[11] Jesus, in his *humanity* on the cross, cried out to God and may have felt abandoned. He wasn't. On the third day, God gave us the most important part of the story we are to tell.

When we freely and wholeheartedly share our dependence upon God and our trust in God, we invite our friends to be open and honest with us. If they are confident enough in themselves and have trust in us, they will do so. And when they do, a yellow flag will wave—that's to caution us to keep confidential everything they tell us. When people share their experiences, emotions, beliefs, or hopes, which are clearly intended only for *our* ears, we need to be extremely careful that we do not inadvertently violate their trust by sharing it with anyone else.[12] This should not prevent us, however, from helping them connect with and relate to other believers. We should invite and bring them to church. Hopefully, in time, others in our faith family will have opportunities to witness to our friends, supporting and adding to the authenticity of what we have shared with them.

Making an Impact by Means of Faith Sharing

A primary focus of this study is learning how to practice the biblical art of hospitality. As we recognize and trust the Spirit of Christ working in us, we need to also recognize the presence of Christ in others, even if they are not yet aware of that presence. One main purpose of church hospitality is to help them become aware. I hope this book will serve many purposes, practical and spiritual. If I tried to capsulize them all into one, calling upon Henri Nouwen's quote again would come very close. Ensure that, "It is the Christ in you, who recognizes the Christ in me."[13] As we speak to others about *our* faith discoveries, they may then discover and welcome the same transforming love of Christ in *their* lives. And should the instant arrive when they realize that Jesus is truly within them, what a "joyous jolt" they will receive!

Telling the very best of what we have experienced from God is faith sharing. Thinking we don't know enough about the Bible can cause anxiety, but we need not be a Bible scholar to talk about our memorable moments with God. Faith sharing is actively loving, listening, and earning the right to tell our story. Here are some tools in review:

- *Continue to grow your faith*: Invest in Bible study, personal devotions, prayer, and worship with others. The Spirit will equip you.
- *Learn to listen*: Practice being attentive when others are speaking. A proverb from my grandmother is helpful—"God gave you two ears and one mouth. Listen twice as much as you talk."
- *Never argue about faith*: N. T. Wright said, "Arguments about God are like pointing a flashlight toward the sky to see if the sun is shining."[14] They are totally nonproductive.

- *Show concern*: Do small acts of kindness. People don't care what you believe until they believe that you care.
- *Ask open-ended questions*: What did you believe as a child? What is your experience with churches and Christians? What made you feel that way?
- *Tell your story*: Describe times that you felt God's love and presence. Share briefly when you decided to be a follower of Jesus and why. Be sure to report recent God sightings and God moments. People may not believe what you believe, but they can never deny your experiences.
- Turn on your *GPS*: Genuinely relate, Pray, Share. Keep going!

Faith Sharing as a Group Ministry

Lunchtime Share Pray (LSP) for Chambersburg is a group consisting of Christian ministers, laity servants, and community leaders. They meet monthly to share with and support one another in ministry, especially praying for God's kingdom to come and God's will to be done in the community. This group represents over twenty different Christian traditions worshipping as one in Christ!

Led by the Spirit, they plan and pursue projects where connection and cooperation with the community can happen. Encouragement to continue these various activities has come, in part, from a discovery by a prayer-filled woman in the group. She brought to our attention an earlier group ministry, Fulton Street Noontime Prayer and Revival of 1857–58.

Over 150 years ago, Christians from an assortment of denominational backgrounds created an environment for unified prayer in a downtown church every day at noon. They had simple, specific rules to maintain their unity. The idea became very popular in New York City, spreading from church to church. It expanded into other areas of the nation and the world beyond, as recorded by Talbot W. Chambers in his book *The New York City Noon Prayer Meeting, A Simple Prayer Gathering That Changed the World*. His firsthand account of that event was published in 1858.[15]

In our town, new people are connecting with an established group that engages in a prayer walk through a chosen area. From multiple congregations, the group gathers weekly to walk one hour while praying for all the people collectively, for businesses to prosper, and for churches to be vital. We also lift up injustice and systemic need within the community and explore ways God is leading us to become part of the solution.

Acknowledging the diversity of dwelling places and people, we speak to those we encounter, making meaningful small talk. The opportunity frequently arises to ask, "Would you like us to pray for you?" Many say yes. Even for those who decline, God's love has been shared, and *that's* good news!

On one of our prayer walks, we encountered drippings of blood from a shooting the previous night. We prayed "the blood of Jesus for all the people involved in the shooting."

Realize and Accept Limitations

Every act of love bears fruit, even if we do not see the resulting evidence of that love. We must understand that not every faith-sharing experience or extended friendship will reveal a spiritual awakening. Our friendship may simply plant seeds. Remember the mustard seed is very small, but it holds great potential.[16] Others may water the seeds we have planted.[17] Just because we don't see signs of faith as a result of our sharing doesn't mean it is not effective. It is most important to remember that much love is shared in befitting words and helpful deeds.

Some people we befriend may have situations that call for skills and expertise we do not have. Professional counseling will be needed for those who are suicidal; persons involved in alcohol or drug abuse; individuals dealing with sexually transmitted or untreated diseases; people suffering from physical, emotional, or sexual abuse; and those who are confronted with legal or complicated problems.

We continue to be their friend, regularly asking how we can pray *for* them and *with* them. We consistently invite and, yes, bring them to worship. This emphasizes that a church family is meant to be a source of welcome and support. Additionally, in a household of faith, those who help others are now on their team, able to pass along more loving care from a spirit of compassion.

Specifically search for places that offer assistance in your friends' areas of need. Be gentle but persistent in reminding them to take the necessary steps to get the expert help they need. Accompanying them to an appointment is a display of love; it may also be necessary. But we should not attempt to help with problems where we are in over our heads.[18]

One day while in the midst of writing this section, I received a call from a friend who had been struggling with addictions. (It is amazing how God fit all of this together.) My friend and I had spent less time together recently. Realizing I was not being as helpful as I had hoped, I continued to pray for her and did small acts of kindness. Then, over the phone came these words: "I was very angry with you because I knew you were right." I had urged her to seek professional help. A grandson led her to a Christian counselor. The call was to tell me of her journey toward recovery and to ask for my presence and prayers with her for a serious medical procedure the next day. I say again, "God *is* amazing." And the response God wants from us ...

Just Do It!

And so we must. It is the same bidding John Wesley gave to those he was leading three hundred years ago: "Begin, oh just Begin!" The movement he began had a profound effect, bringing many from outside the church into its embrace. It was the start of what is now over seventy faith traditions throughout the world, rooted in Wesleyan soil, from which thousands of people have been nurtured and gathered for God's kingdom on earth.

As we continue in a friendship and become willing, God will open a door at an appropriate time and give us the opportunity to share our stories. Just imagine what God will do with our faithfulness. Yes, we must keep driving to show our friends who Jesus is, but we are to follow God's good and patient lead—carefully being real, not phony; talking *with* them, not at or over them; and loving, not judging; pleasing God.

For me, hearing how Christ is overflowing in someone's life is most powerful. From the experiences of Frank Laubach, a renowned literacy educator and world missionary, I have learned to better practice the presence of God. Laubach's words have been both challenging and encouraging. He wrote of the wonderful benefit of dwelling in God's presence: "It becomes easy to tell others about Christ because our minds are flooded with him, out of the fullness of the heart the mouth speaks."[19] Just simply tell about the times we felt close to God.

There are people you know and those you have yet to meet. Some are like you, and some are very different. God is calling you and me to build relationships with them in loving and authentic ways. With God's help at just the right time, you will be able to smile and tell a simple story of how you have experienced the living God. Then you can say, "That's what I believe. What do you believe?" No matter the name—witnessing, faith sharing, "fishing"—you can do it!

Hospitality Challenge

1. Think about and develop your faith story. Sketch it on a three-by-five card, as I described earlier under "A Threefold Sketch of My Faith Story." You can use both sides of the card to illustrate three different stages of your life when you experienced the love of God. If you can discern the time you decided to follow Jesus, note it as the apex of your faith journey. Fold and keep the card in your wallet, where you are sure to see it. It will be a reminder of the big moments God worked in your life—a reminder that you do indeed have a story to share.

2. a. Recall a hard time in your life that had the most meaningful, positive effect on your relationship with God.
    b. Then think of when you questioned God's presence or response during an extreme difficulty.
    c. Consider sharing one or both of your stories (a and b, above) with someone who is currently going through a painful situation. Choose what you think will best move them toward God. Offer to pray with the person as well.

3. Faith steps that help draw people into a closer relationship with Jesus:
    a) Pray for a willingness to engage in friendship evangelism.
    b) Ask God to open your eyes to new friends.
    c) Depend upon God to teach you how to love, listen, and earn your friends' trust.
    d) Pray for inspiration and authority to naturally and boldly tell your story when God says, "You're on."
    e) Invite and bring your friend to worship services and other circles of Christian relationships: one-on-ones with more church-family members, small groups, Sunday school, Bible study, ministries.
    f) When you feel the time is right and believe you have received God's confirmation, ask your friend, "Would you like to welcome Jesus into your life?"
    g) Whatever the answer, pray with your friend accordingly.
    h) Seek God's guidance for how to continue the relationship.

4. In what ways can we recognize the presence of Christ in people? When circumstances allow, discuss this question with others.

5. As we try to catch people to tell them about Jesus and his love, what is meant by "Sometimes the best fishing is upstream, working against the current"? This too is worthy of discussion.

6. Consider joining with other Christians from various traditions in your community to develop prayer walks and other faith-sharing events.

Prayer

Jesus, remind me often that people need to hear of your great love and that you are asking me to share my experiences of that love. I want to be willing. Help me help others come to know you. Amen.

CHAPTER 11

The Least and the Lost Are Loved by God, So We Convey God's Love for Them

'Lord, when did we ever see you hungry and feed you? Or thirsty and give you something to drink? Or a stranger and show you hospitality?' … And the King will say, 'I tell you the truth, when you did it to one of the least of these my brothers and sisters, you were doing it to me!'
—Matthew 25:37–38, 40 (NLT)

The first time I met Allen was on a Sunday morning. I was hurrying to assist in the next worship service when a young teen ran after me, saying someone needed to talk. Upon reaching Allen, he began, "I guess you don't have time for me now, but I really need the Lord in my life, and I was hoping you could pray with me." I felt strongly that God wanted me to drop everything and share time with Allen. A brief explanation to the lead pastor cleared the way.

Allen had come to First United Methodist Church with friends who were regular attendees at the Thursday community supper and service. As we headed to the chapel, his tears began to flow. Kneeling at the altar, he wanted to be released from anger. While counseling had helped, he wanted more—to be forgiven, to be changed. He knew he needed the Lord to help him.

Through tears of regret, there was a moment of surrender. Then a spirit of love welcomed him as a full member of God's family. Jesus' gift of forgiveness heralded the birth of Allen's new life. That was the beginning of my friendship with Allen. It continued with us having many conversations. Topics ranged from needing assistance with the basics of life to having assurance from our Bible discussions.

During this time, his friend Carolyn, who had invited and introduced Allen to the church, became his girlfriend and then his fiancée. They and some of their friends wanted to be baptized. On Pentecost, sporting new red T-shirts and shorts, they all knelt before the congregation; each received holy baptism. Church membership was next. Now they belonged not only to God's family but to the First United Methodist family. Every Thursday and every Sunday, they were present at church.

Before long, we started pre-marital sessions, building relationship tools that would help their marriage become lasting. Their words to me were, "We want a church wedding. We want to do it right this time!" For a year, they planned their day—made payments on the gown; rented tuxedos; lined up a full wedding party; and together crafted silk-flower bouquets and table arrangements. A ceremony of praise music and favorite scriptures all culminated in the church wedding of their dreams. A full-course meal reception—sponsored, prepared, and served by church members—concluded their special day.

Thirty-three days after the dream wedding, Allen had a massive stroke. Once again, the church was there, standing by his hospital bed. Despite the severe pain from his illness, Allen had an assurance that he was surrounded by God's presence. Within a week, he died. After his memorial service, a church member responded, "Allen is experiencing life eternal because of the commitment First United Methodist has to be in ministry with the poor."

The church family became essential in helping Carolyn pick up the pieces of her once-again broken life. The memorial service and luncheon were laced with love and spiritual nourishment, financial support, offers of assistance with relocation, and suggestions for an income that would help meet basic expenses. A few church members began having Carolyn do house cleaning for them. Even with disabilities, she worked very hard and continued to manage challenging circumstances. She was making it with the help of her church family.

There are many Allens and Carolyns in the world. They are in my community and your community, visible with open natural eyes, though often not so visible with closed spiritual ones. But God's heart yearns to have intimate relationships with all of them, just as he does with you and me—everyone. That is why God calls all churches to be in ministry *with*, not just *to*, the poor. God is making an appeal for them through us, the church. We are to show them God in us.

God's Spirit continually nudges us to keep our spiritual eyes open so we can seek out the Allens and the Carolyns and find ways to help them experience the fullness of God. We are to be *ambassadors for Christ*, establishing relationships with the poor, founded on acceptance, love, and forgiveness. We must talk with them, not just to or about them. We need to earn their trust and dare to trust them. We serve them best by utilizing all appropriate means to ensure they have adequate food, clothing, and shelter. Most important, we must abide by the message and ministry of reconciliation. Just as God made us right with him (saved us) through Christ, we are to share the good news with the poor (by any definition) that they too can be made right with God through Christ (2 Corinthians 5:18–20 NLT). Each can experience fully God's personal acceptance, love, and forgiveness.

Class, Clothes, and Cash

Churches in our Western culture are often composed primarily of white middle-class Americans. Because God loves everyone, God's heart pounds for all who feel intimidated by becoming part of what is foreign to their experience and resources. Something as simple as not having anything to put in the offering plate is an example of why the poor may stay away. They know who they are, how they dress, and what they have, and they tend to measure themselves as less. *They need to know how God measures them!*

It is not unusual to adopt an us-or-them mentality regarding the rich, middle class, and poor. Those of *us* in the church, however, are called to respond to God's desire to include *them*. Remember it takes great courage for them to overcome any stigma from the C's (class, clothes, and cash) and come among us. When they do, we must be ready to overcome our discomforts from their presence with us. It means walking up to one of "the least and the lost," looking him or her in the eye, and offering the person a seat beside us. If we reach that point, we have started to *get it*.

Embracing the Scriptures That Embrace the Poor

The drumbeat of hospitality is heard when we respond by living out the love God has for us. Scripture challenges us *and* shows us how. As believers, we want to live by the scriptures. Yet we often find it difficult to love those who are like us and—even more demanding—to love those who are not. But we must acknowledge there are specific instructions on how to relate to those caught in the clutches of poverty. There are more than two thousand verses in scripture that refer to the poor. Here are just a few we often miss:

- "However, there should be no poor among you, for in the land the LORD your God is giving you to possess as your inheritance, he will richly bless you, if only you fully obey the LORD your God and are careful to follow all these commands I am giving you today" (Deuteronomy 15:4–5 NIV).
- "If you help the poor, you are lending to the Lord—and he will repay you!" (Proverbs 19:17 NLT).
- "Whoever gives to the poor will lack nothing, but the one who turns a blind eye will get many a curse" (Proverbs 28:27 NRSV).
- "Listen, my beloved brothers and sisters. Has not God chosen the poor in the world to be rich in faith and to be heirs of the kingdom that he has promised to those who love him? But you have dishonored the poor. Is it not the rich who oppress you? Is it not they who drag you into court? Is it not they who blaspheme the excellent name that was invoked over you?" (James 2:5–7 NRSV).

Jesus Has Good News for All—the Least, the Lost, and the Last Come First

Jesus, a Hebrew, came with a message not only for Israel but for every individual—Jews, Gentiles, men, women, children, the rich, the poor, everyone! For God, it was not about nation or gender or socioeconomic standing; it was about *each* person.

God with us is who Jesus was. Beginning in the synagogue at Nazareth with his mission statement, noting from Isaiah, Jesus declared, "The Lord's Spirit has come to me, because he has chosen me to tell the good news to the poor. The Lord has sent me to announce freedom for prisoners, to give sight to the blind, to free everyone who suffers" (Luke 4:18 CEV). During the rest of his time on earth, Jesus reached out to all people to build the kingdom of God. Jesus came to his own people, but he expanded the invitation to everyone, including lepers, community outcasts, sinners of every description, and the poor. As Jesus traveled throughout the land, his teachings focused on loving all others and inviting them to come be part of God's kingdom.

In this kingdom, people recognize they are loved by God, turn from their ungodly ways, and live the royal law to love God in return and love neighbor as self. Every neighbor is to be loved. It doesn't matter how different or motley they are, nor how far from God's way they have wandered. And truly, *everyone* is our neighbor. Jesus purposely called specific attention to the needy because he was aware of how easy it is to overlook the invisible poor.

In choosing his disciples, Jesus conversed with God all night. Surprisingly, Jesus selected some unlikely folks. These twelve disciples, with whom He spent quality time and developed intimate relationships, were mostly of low income and uneducated. It was these folks Jesus would entrust with carrying on the message of the kingdom.[1] Imagine turning over to lower-class persons the plan to bring many more into an intimate relationship with God. Yet Jesus chose these ordinary people to work most closely with him in building the kingdom of God.

Throughout his ministry, Jesus connected with person after person, who some religious leaders avoided, calling attention to those who were considered unacceptable. This intentional reaching out was a clear testament that the kingdom of God is for everyone. Jesus didn't stand apart from the least of these and give them advice: He touched them.[2] Jesus spent much time with them. He included them. He loved them.

As Jesus was preparing to leave this earth, at a private dinner with his disciples, he gave this diverse, unlikely group of followers a new commandment that they must love each other.[3] He was insistent, even demanding, that they "love each other as I have loved you" (John 15:12 NIV). The twelve intimate followers of Jesus were called to demonstrate to the entire world the same kind of love they had received from him.

Then Jesus described this self-emptying love: "No one has greater love than this, that someone would lay down his life for his friends" (John 15:13 HCSB). Jesus would give us the greatest love the world would ever know by laying down his very life. Jesus charged his followers to love everyone that much.

In Jesus' last recorded teaching to the masses, Matthew 25, which can be considered his farewell address, he declared judgment upon those who did not serve the least of these. Jesus stated that in the final judgment, we will be judged on how we fed the hungry, gave drink to the thirsty, clothed the naked, visited the sick and imprisoned, and welcomed the stranger. He concluded with, "Truly I tell you, just as you did not do it to one of the least of these, you did not do it to me. And these will go away into eternal punishment, but the righteous into eternal life" (Matthew 25:45–46 NRSV).

Highly significant is that Jesus did not say, "Don't serve anyone who takes advantage of you or is ungrateful." In fact, earlier in his ministry, he established the intentions for us: "But love your enemies, do good and lend, expecting nothing in return. Your reward will be great, and you will be children of the Most High; for he (God) is kind to the ungrateful and the wicked. Be merciful, just as your Father is merciful" (Luke 6:35–36 NIV).

Why does Jesus highlight the needy stranger? Jesus wants us to understand that *serving the needy stranger* is central to our understanding of the Christian faith. In serving, we humble ourselves and become as a servant. This is Jesus work; he is the suffering servant. Those who follow are called to live out such servant love. "Needy stranger" is a brand upon our hearts as a reminder to welcome the stranger and serve the needy. Jesus wants those who bear both labels to minister to each. The kingdom of God is for everyone.

All of this paying God's love forward may seem like just too much. But God is amazing with paybacks. When God asks something of us, the Holy Spirit, with whom we can trust the outcome, comes to us. Our part is obedience, which invokes the Spirit. Indeed, doing what Jesus asks creates incredible God moments. Theologian Parker J. Palmer strongly expounds throughout his writing that when lives are touched by experiencing the Spirit, both the life touched and the one touching are changed. From this he concludes our society will be changed for the better.[4] I firmly agree and believe that best of all, the one touched just may surrender to the transforming love of God in Christ Jesus—and the kingdom grows!

Saul Became the Apostle Paul

Saul, a learned scholar and member of the upper stratum of society, understood well the Hebrew scriptures of welcoming the stranger and helping the poor. Jesus had come, not to abandon the law but to fulfill the Old Testament law of loving God and loving neighbor. Paul, having been transformed into an apostle, tried to live out the fullness of Jesus. With Jesus' love, Paul's example, and the power of the Spirit, we can do likewise.

Paul became a missionary and a "church planter." As an enlightened follower of Jesus, Paul knew if you have not reached out to those in prison, those who need clothes, and those who are hungry, then you have not fully served Jesus. Paul followed the example of the first Christian church, having everything in common, and urged partnerships and inclusion of all socioeconomic types in the churches that resulted from his missionary efforts.[5]

In Galatians, the story is recorded of a man who was invited as a coworker by the leaders of the church in Jerusalem. They were concentrating their ministry on the Jews. To expand the kingdom, they wanted Paul to share the good news with the Gentiles. In relating this story, Paul points out, "All they asked was that we should continue to remember the poor, the very thing I was eager to do" (Galatians 2:10 NIV). Remember the poor? Absolutely! Paul practiced their care and instructed the newly formed churches to follow his lead. To the Christians at Corinth, he pushed for a partnership: "I do not mean that there should be relief for others and pressure on you, but it is a question of a fair balance between your present abundance and their need so that their abundance may be for your need" (2 Corinthians 8:13–14 NRSV). In current jargon, we could say that in serving each other, we serve both the haves and the have-nots.

Mother Teresa's Call

Mother Teresa, a canonized saint in the Catholic Church was believed to be a true disciple of Jesus Christ by Catholics and Protestants; even unbelievers acknowledged the authenticity of this humble, devoted servant of God. Called to a life of full-time commitment and obedience, including personal poverty and chastity, she became Sister Teresa. Initially, her appointment was as a teacher and later, headmistress to a school in Calcutta, India. After nearly two decades in that mission, she heard Jesus calling her to a ministry with the poor and neglected. I was a director of Christian education at the time I read of her response, and it was very meaningful, even transforming, for me.[6]

Uncovering Mother Teresa's ministry of carrying the love and peace of Jesus to those who were caught in the clutches of poverty increased my own convictions of the way people caught in such bondage were neglected by the church. It grew clearer to me how Jesus longs to be in relationships with the forgotten and ignored and asks *us* to carry his love to them. Pondering how we do that in our current church culture pulsed through my veins.[7]

Enlightenment for the Contemporary Church

Gaining inspiration from Mother Teresa's example while unwrapping my own call, I needed— and yes, the church would need—to remain in loving contact with God through prayer. It is true that such work cannot be properly understood outside the context of a prayer life.[8]

For churches of the Western world to do the work of Christ, we must hear again the words of Christ.

Come, you that are blessed by the Father, inherit the kingdom prepared for you from the foundation of the world. ... I was hungry ... I was thirsty ... I was a stranger ... I was naked ... I was sick ... I was in prison. (Matthew 25:34b-36 NRSV)

"When?" we asked.

When you gave me food ... you gave me something to drink ... you welcomed me ... you gave me clothing ... you took care of me ... you visited me. (Matthew 25: 35-36 NRSV)

"*You?*" we asked.
And Jesus responds with this challenge:

Truly I tell you, just as you did it to one of the least of these who are members of my family, you did it to me. (Matthew 25:40b NRSV)

We struggle with Jesus' challenge because the very people we often try to avoid are to be Christ for us. We are to treat them as if they are Christ!

Life in our rich Western Hemisphere is entangled by materialism, laws, programs, insurances, privacy acts, and myriad other red-tape issues. Many in our society find it very difficult to muster the time, the energy, and the inclination to show poor people that someone loves them.[9]

Loving the Poor Is Kingdom Work

Showing love is not simply offering people a handout or teaching them how to behave. Instead, our every response to any situation should display sincere care and concern for all involved. If someone causes a disturbance that is not easily settled, calling the police may be the best expression of love. But calling them to remove someone just because the person isn't one of us denies that person love. Jesus calls us to do kingdom work—work of the heart—wanting every individual to experience God's forgiving, transforming love. Such love comes to us from Jesus and is intended to flow through us on its way to others. When we ensure that it gets there, we have surrendered to God's will. We are to love people into the kingdom of God.

The church, consisting of followers of Jesus, is the only community that offers God's love. While our government does provide programs with resources to supply basic needs, such programs alone will rarely release people from poverty. No government alone can do kingdom work. God's plan is that the obedient church will receive the Holy Spirit to help us with this crucial task. When we, as Christians, open ourselves to the Spirit, the amazing grace of God abounds. We become enlightened, enthused, energized, and eager to love. God's kingdom comes, and God's will is done—on earth as it is in heaven.

Challenging, Messy Work

Churches often do not like to minister at the poverty level of kingdom work. In the words of one pastor, such ministry is *messy*.[10] The least of these are persons who lack sufficient resources in several areas: financial income, mental ability, mental wellness, family nurture, work ethic, support, and love. With these deficiencies come baggage and issues. Knowing we need to lead and guide such folks in the orderly ways of God, the church can't expect them to readily act like *church people.* Any notion we have of being parental and bringing them in line with our middle-class mores will only manifest itself as middle-class snobbery. The love Jesus came to bring them through us will be lost in our attempt to control.

So often their problems are made worse by bad choices. We show our love when we help them make good ones. We can explain, suggest, encourage—even implore—but we should resist the impulse to compel; it's up to them. And for their smart decisions, we celebrate with them in love and joy!

When Jesus calls us to follow, the call is to offer the kingdom of God to everyone. A wise bishop once said, "If every Christian was a real friend to one poor person in our world, we could eliminate poverty." Thus, the question each Christian must ask is, "Am I a real friend to a poor person?"

From such friendships, enduring relationships may be built. In our association with the poor, we can carry the love of Jesus to them. By providing this love, "We have earned the right to be heard" (the ministry model of Young Life leaders). We can help hearts become unlocked doors—be ajar, open wide—and understand and believe John 3:16 for themselves.

In speaking with a friend one day, I remembered our conversation about some people who were really in need of God's love in their lives. They were, however, not making it easy to shower them with love. These folks clearly qualified as EGR people—extra grace required.

EGR means more patience, time, effort, and "paper towels" are needed to clear a way for love to get through and take hold. But God has plenty of grace for any messy relationship and any strained commitment. When we remember being called through scripture to love because God first loved us, we are restored in strength and determination. We want to help all persons experience the life-redeeming love of Jesus. That love will enable them to better recognize and use God's good gifts throughout their lives. We want them to grow in ways that please God. They may never be spotless on the outside, but God wants them spick-and-span on the inside.

Do We Really Believe God's Love Is Intended for Everyone?

Perhaps you remember the story *The Hunchback of Notre Dame*. For the Disney movie based on the novel, composers Alan Menken and Stephen Schwartz wrote a song, "God Help the Outcasts." Here are partial lyrics in the song and responses for us to consider if we believe God's love is intended for everyone.

> God help the outcasts, hungry from birth.
> The lost and forgotten, they look to You still.
> God help the outcasts or nobody will.
> … the tattered, the torn,
> Winds of misfortune have blown them about. The poor and unlucky, the weak and the odd,
> I thought we all were the children of God.[11]

God chooses to help the outcasts through Christians in the church, to show mercy they don't frequently find on this earth. As partners with God, we are to remember and then reassure them we are all children of God, created in God's image. Offering the hope of Jesus to the seemingly hopeless and the apparently helpless is how the kingdom is built. If we do not do it, nobody will.

Churches that embrace kingdom work find it fulfilling: They experience the closeness of God while becoming equipped. Yet they still acknowledge the many challenges that come with the task. Having personally heard a call to extend God's hospitality to the least of these, I can attest to how messy it is at times. Jesus is surely present at every moment and occasion in which we impart God's love to others. But the devil often shows up as well.

Each of us and every church must answer two very important questions: Do we really believe in the forgiving, renewing love of Jesus? And if yes, do we truly believe this love is intended for everyone—from the rich and the famous to the least and the lost, from the most innocent child to the most wicked offender?

Hopefully, our answers are analogous to "We *do* believe God's love is merciful, re-creative, and all inclusive." If so, we must press on, messy or not, and find ways to show people that someone loves them—radically. This kind of love magnifies the kingdom of God.

Churches That Touch All Types of People

Many people want to help contemporary churches do ministry with the least and the lost. One who touches lives in his community the way Jesus touched lives is Rudy Rasmus. His inner-city church in Houston has grown from a failing church with a large facility but few members to a thriving church, where the homeless and outcasts sit alongside the middle class and the fabulously wealthy. Pastor Rudy accepts each person with God's great love. He watches as that love mightily changes lives.

In his book *Touch: The Power of Touch in Transforming Lives*, Rasmus expresses some practical truths that must be implemented for God's grace and empowerment to work most effectively. He simply writes,

> My book doesn't offer steps or secret formulas to success. I can only point you to Jesus and encourage you to get real with Him. When that happens, a revolution takes place in your heart! It's a transformation that is more powerful and deep than any formula can promise. Then, his love and strength flow through you to touch the hearts of hurting people around you—and in case you didn't know it that includes everybody.

Because others have been involved in such ministries, you need not invent the ways to begin. Hopefully, you will find some of Pastor Rudy's proven principles helpful.

- People who come to our churches and are different from us will soon be labeled "those people." It is not just a good thing to reach out to the marginalized; we will need to defend their right to be there (17).
- Caring for people the way Jesus cared for people involves real risks (25).
- People respond to each other in one of two ways: in fear or in love. Fear is at the heart of exclusion, and fear perpetuates our desire to be distant from people who aren't like us. Love is a tremendously powerful force (19). As Christians we are reminded, "Perfect love casts out fear" (1 John 4:18 NRSV).
- We must reach out to people other churches don't want or to people who, for some reason, don't feel comfortable in other churches (45).
- The true test of our love is our affection and action to help "the least of these" who can never repay our kindness, but our wells run dry pretty quickly unless they are replenished by the constant flow of God's love in our own experience (51).
- Do the Jesus thing: love people with a full heart, and let them respond any way they choose (79).
- Jesus' goal wasn't to categorize them into believers and unbelievers, clean and unclean, righteous and unrighteous. He met each person where they were and tried to bring them to the center of God's presence so they could experience his love (86).
- We simply can't have a real ministry to "the least of these" if we are afraid to touch people (124).[12]

Rudy speaks of his works of service:

> I love to see God use me to change lives, but I don't live for that. I live for His smile. Over and over again, I think of Jesus' explanation of the reward of following Him: "His master said to him, 'Well done, good and faithful servant; you have been faithful over a few things, I will make you ruler over many things. Enter into the joy of your master'" (Matthew 25:21 MEV).

And I can feel his touch.[13]

Joy in Serving the Least

Since Jesus is the stranger and the least of these, if we followers are to live as he has taught us, we must *serve* the least of these. Parker Palmer pointed out such changes in roles and hearts when he wrote, "The stranger is not simply one who needs us. We need the stranger. We need the stranger if we are to know Christ and serve God, in truth and in love. For it is only by knowing the truth and by serving in love that we ourselves will be set free."[14] Serving the least of these is part of our salvation journey. It is a great and good sign of our gratitude for the gift of salvation. We are all able to make God smile.

Such joy happens! In a church that through the years has sponsored a community supper and service that was keyed on the poor, one spring evening nine people were baptized in Christ. In this service were tears, smiles, hugs, and a sense of belonging. It was a time to celebrate the new beginning that comes when the grace of the Father, Son, and Holy Spirit falls upon God's children.

Only one of these people was employed; he worked part-time. A single mom, with four delightful children, was involved in a program to help her find a job. There were those with pressing mental or physical health issues, some with mental retardation, a former prisoner, and several recovering from addiction. As Lupton wrote, "The work of harvesting good grain is never far from the infestation of troublesome tares."[15]

While the lives of these nine people may not have seemed as fruitful as for many Christians, and the challenges they had to overcome were many, their faith was real. Clearly, becoming a member of God's family was a wonderful, holy experience for all nine of these children of God.

The church continued to love and include them. It helped them grow, even if ever so slowly or if there were setbacks. Nine people have life eternal, and God smiles. The kingdom has been advanced, and the community is a slightly better place to live. God used the Christians of that church to offer them Christ—and they accepted!

Churches That Do Not Touch All Types of People

A newspaper editorial, "Some Churches Need More Warmth," written by George R. Plagenz, criticized some attempts—or not—at church hospitality. He reported that John Charles Thomas Jr. had visited 195 churches over a three-year period. Mr. Thomas noted that the most hospitality he had received was from a dog that wandered into a worship service. Without reservation, the hospitable canine came and licked his hand before lying down at his feet.

The article went on to say that Thomas's many occasions of *terrible church hospitality* were his reasons for not regularly attending any church. The author concluded with a stinging story that indicted Christians for not welcoming a stranger:

> In a small town, a woman was very concerned about her wayward brother. He had just returned from reform school. She finally convinced him to come with her to church. During the service, his heart was deeply touched; and at the end of the service, he went and knelt at the altar. Not one single person went to be with him or even acknowledged his repentant spirit. He left that church feeling very rejected, telling his sister he would never again enter a church. He never did. So, John Dillinger instead became Public Enemy #1.[16]

Mr. Thomas felt very strongly the church had failed to offer God's hospitality. His own personal experience supported that resolve. He cited additional examples of animals being welcome in a church. God doesn't expect that of us—but failing to welcome a person? Had John Dillinger been enfolded by the congregation, sharing the love of God that is most complete in Jesus' forgiveness, would John's life have been different? We can only wonder and hope the answer is *yes*.

Jesus Touches Still

When a church accepts and loves the least of these, as Jesus did, many of the people we serve will be on the bottom layer of the world. There will be John Dillingers who come. But when we give the love of Jesus, we are promised that lives will be changed. It is the only real hope for the reformation of *their* world—*this* world. Love is God's way of bringing people into the kingdom.

God's kingdom is not of this world, but it is *in* this world. God wants an abundant life for all people, here and now and forever more. When we help others to know and feel God's love through our love, we help to arm them spiritually for eternity and practically for today. As their relationship with God grows, they become more confident and capable of dealing with life's problems, because they become more reliant on God's promise and provision.

Ministering with the least and the lost (not simply *to* them) will likely remain messy work, but it will always be Messianic work. We must remember the words of Jesus: "Whatever you did not do for the least of these, you did not do for me" (Matthew 25:45 NRSV). Just as Jesus touched our lives with his love, we are to touch the lives of others with our love. Relationships connected by love are key. We are to be the hands and feet of Jesus. We are to have and be the very heart of Christ the Lord.

Hospitality Challenge

1. Many ministries with the poor can be part of your congregation's outreach. Providing food or clothing for them is a good initial way to enact God's love and to welcome them into your church. Consider the following not-for-profit happenings in the church or conducted by the congregation outside of your church:
   - meals with devotions, weekly or monthly
   - grocery bags with personal, friendly interaction
   - coffee, pastries, and conversation
   - clothing ministry: all types of clothing or a specialty, like shoes and boots, children's clothing, men's clothing
   - after-school children's ministry that includes ministry with the parents
   - neighborhood teen ministry
2. Think of two examples that illustrate the difference between ministering *to* the poor and ministering *with* the poor. Share your examples with someone.
3. Whenever we interact with EGR folks, remember that *we* are EGR folks to God.
4. a. Have you ever been touched by spiritual love from another and felt the presence of God?
   b. Have you touched someone with such love and known God's presence?
   c. Do these experiences shed light on loving "the least and the lost"? If yes, step into the light and allow it to reflect your love upon all others. If not, keep seeking the light!

Prayer: Sit quietly, and imagine Jesus is sitting with you. Ask him this question:

"Lord, when did we ever see you hungry or thirsty or a stranger or naked or sick or in prison, and not help you?" 'And he will answer, "I tell you the truth, when you refused to help the least of these my brothers and sisters, you were refusing to help me."' (Matthew 25:44–45 NLT)

Can you now pray this prayer by Dan Schutte?

Here I am, Lord. Is it I, Lord? I have heard you calling in the night.
I will go, Lord, if you lead me. I will hold your people in my heart. [17]

AFTERWORD

Launching God's Love

There is so much more to say. After twenty years of teaching, preaching, and writing on God's hospitality, my learning continues as I uncover more about the hospitality God intended from the beginning. I love to learn, tell the story, and hear how lives have been touched.

Recently in a concert, a marvelous piano improvisation of Scott Joplin's "Pineapple Rag" created images of jazzy Southern hospitality—beautiful, inviting, bounteous, and delicious; powerfully engaging. Over the years, the pineapple has symbolized all these attributes of hospitality. Listening, I heard joy as I imagined the hosts and party-goers intermingling, interrelating. I smiled as I watched the pianist passionately rise ever so slightly from the bench to awaken the keys, opening the movement to superb harmonious hospitality.

God's hospitality has roused that kind of joy and passion in my heart. What I know for certain is that God put that passion within me. It's broader and deeper than the most splendid pineapple hospitality. I *must* sound out God's song. It is invigorating; it lifts me from my seat. It is life-changing. And, quite honestly, it is distinctly challenging, but I am always drawn back to the Composer and then to the keyboard: "Love so amazing, so divine, demands my life, my soul, my all."

I've made mistakes, and much like the pianist, I have found it necessary to rethink and re-create how I play out my beliefs and practices. But despite my human condition and limitations, I still yearn to be part of God's hospitality chorus, stirring many more hearts, minds, souls, and churches. Hopefully, God has been tapping, even striking, the keys of *your* soul.

As you concluded chapter 11, you read, "Just as Jesus touched our lives with *his* love, we are to touch the lives of others with *our* love. Relationships connected by love are key." So the church is to embrace its relentless, divine call to launch God's love into our wandering world. God pursues gifted Christians for leadership and fellowship in ministries that welcome and connect people to such great love.

God Has Gifted Us All

Do you remember Eric from this book's introduction? He did not consider himself hospitable; it was a sincere and "gifted" evaluation. Though polite and self-assured, he was not gregarious, but he *was* in God's plan. Since Eric is my nephew, I've had the privilege of watching him enter into Christ. Through time, he has become a man who seeks to develop relationships for the sake of the gospel. Eric is passionate about launching ministry and mission that bring others into God's glorious grace.

Eric is unique, but so is each of us. Created by the same love, we have been given different personalities and gifts to provide love in different ways. We are to love and serve God by loving and serving people—uniquely—as God has planned. Our readiness is a heart open to hear God's call and a faith determined to follow God's lead. Through experience and spiritual growth, we can learn to appreciate and apply our special gifts. With God's help, all of us are capable of launching into a lifestyle that invites others to come, connect, and belong to the family of God.

Like God's, does my heart hunger to bring others to the kingdom?

God's Kingdom—Our Hospitality

Our Father in heaven ... your kingdom come, your will be done on earth as it is in heaven!

Every person on this earth has a good, good Father. You and I are loved by that good, good Father. It is who we are: beloved children of God! With this realization, God asks me to respond by doing all to affirm and demonstrate that *our* Father's love is for *everyone*. God asks for the same response from *you*. We are to help build God's kingdom by helping to fill God's houses. We begin by being hospitable.

Attend to Scripture—Be Relational

Every person wants to belong. There is a deep desire to be connected in community with others and a deeper need to be connected in communion with God. From the beginning of Genesis to the end of Revelation, we learn that these relationships are to be bonded in God's love—a covenant at creation, confirmed by Christ Jesus, and continued as our calling to work it out in partnership with God and each other. Developing loving relationships with those outside our safe circles can be trying. But by faith in the power of the Spirit, we can overcome the fear of rejection, put the needs of others above our own, and push forward.

Do I attempt to include those not connected with our congregation?

Three Essential Dos

Do invite: Our churches should follow a plan to teach and encourage people to invite and bring others. Churches tend to flourish and bear good fruit when they do; those that don't often wither and die. Invitation can be key to salvation.

Do share faith: Congregations that express and exemplify the goodness of God are sharing their faith. During our daily routines, openings to opportunities often appear. We should be prepared to naturally and lovingly describe to others the joyous presence of God's love in our lives. That may ignite a craving to know God's love in *their* lives. Such stories can draw the one who hears and the one who tells closer to each other and both closer to God.

Do extend hospitality to the least and the lost: "The King will answer, 'Whatever you do to someone (hungry, thirsty, homeless, without clothes, sick, or in prison), you do it to me.'" We are to welcome the least as if they were Jesus. We are to lead the lost into the light of Jesus. We are to be receptive, attentive, trustworthy, and even vulnerable. It can be difficult, messy, unpopular work. But Jesus makes ministry with the poor a priority. Thus, the question remains:

Do I—do we—invite, share faith with, and extend hospitality to the least and the lost?

Depending upon God

For our churches to produce and sustain "healthy hospitality," the love that God plants in us must be continually and faithfully nurtured. This love is meant to unfold into full bloom. We are challenged to give off the refreshing fragrance of God's love—the same pleasing aroma that Jesus shared wherever he went, whomever he was with, whatever he was about.

Jesus was always about serving his Father. And so we ask, "What can *we* do for God?" At first, the answers may seem small and insignificant. But then it occurs to us to ask a slightly different question: "What can God do *through* us?"

> God can do anything, you know—far more than you could ever imagine or guess or request in your wildest dreams! He does it not by pushing us around but by working within us, his Spirit deeply and gently within us. (Ephesians 3:20 MSG)

So we place our hearts, ourselves, and our churches in the hands of God. We are to serve at God's discretion. Our Father gives us a clearer understanding of what it means to "imitate" Christ. Jesus allowed God's lavish love to flow through him; God wants us and our churches to do the same. Are we not called to launch out into a world where people are adrift and disoriented, needing love and help to find the way home?

And we hear God's assurance: "Go; I am with you!"

Glory to God in the church!
Glory to God in the Messiah, in Jesus!
Glory down all the generations!
Glory through all millennia! Oh, yes! (Ephesians 3:21 MSG)

Just imagine—what God can do through you and your church!

HOSPITALITY QUOTIENT

A Self-Evaluation

I hope this book has been and will continue to be a source of knowledge and inspiration for faithfully and effectively providing God's hospitality. We cannot give away what we do not have or truly share what we do not believe. So it is essential to evaluate where we are in our faith journey and consider what God is calling us to do.

This evaluation is intended to be an honest experience between you and God. For each numbered statement below, record a point value based on where you are. Then total your points.

Point Values: I *live* this—3;   I *believe* this—2;   I'm not sure—1;   No, not me—0   **Points**

1. God creates all humans in his image, in his very likeness, and longs for each one to know and accept that they are a child of God. I am a child of God! ____

2. Knowing all are created in God's likeness, I am to imitate God's love to everyone. ____

3. In scripture, God declares that children of God are to welcome the stranger. ____

4. God gives his children Ten Commands how to live and love: four for loving God and six for loving others. I should always obey God's laws of love. ____

5. All fall short of God's plan. That includes me. I am to confess and pray: "Forgive me my sins as I forgive those who sin against me." ____

6. To become a Christian, we respond to Jesus' invitation to "come to me." My salvation is being born anew: Christ in me. ____

7. Since all love comes from God, with Christ in me, I have the power of the Holy Spirit to love even the unlovable and in the most difficult circumstances. ____

8. Being a Christian, I am an ambassador for Christ as I relate to others in word and deed. It is a matter of the heart. I must allow God to make his appeal through me. ____

9. I speak for Christ when I go out of my way to reach out in love, welcoming, inviting, and bringing people into my home, church events, or other activities. As they connect with the family of God, they might also be born from above. ____

10. To follow the example of Christ, who offered himself as a sacrifice, I must share much love with many—be unselfish, kind, and caring; extend God's grace; tell God's stories; and spend time praying with and for others to experience the love of Jesus, including the least of these. I am to become a *little Christ*. _____

What do your separate point values and total score tell you about yourself? Total Score: _____

Ask God to help you move forward in your faith journey, listening and preparing for your call.

ACKNOWLEDGMENTS

Edward Wentz has journeyed with me in sharing God's hospitality for nearly fifteen years. He made valuable contributions as a member of the small group that supported my doctor of ministry project: "The Church Relearning God's Hospitality to Each Other, Visitors, Guests, and Strangers in Our Midst, Especially the Least and the Lost." In writing this book, I asked Ed to read it and offer suggestions. He then volunteered to edit the book. Investing countless hours—days, months, years—through every setback, he reminded me, "This book is to be written; it *will* happen!" Perhaps his greatest contribution is how much he believes in the mission of hospitality and how he has embraced it as a lifestyle for himself.

Judy Young has been a dear, devoted friend for five decades. She has given me untold freedom to be myself as I continue to discover who God intends me to be. There are times she pushes me where I don't want to go—many times allowing me to just stop and stagnate—nevertheless loving me at all times. Judy is a friend who took me to seminars; she also went to seminars, took notes, and then brought them back to me. She is an educator who loves books and is more familiar with them than anyone else I've known. She is a librarian who knows what should and should not be in a book. Judy is also a Christian colleague who has worked faithfully to help create and develop a hospitality team in her congregation.

First readers: Leslie Gotwald is a young wife and mother who formerly found joy in teaching social studies. She has recently felt a call to ministry. Having many gifts and a passion to challenge believers to become disciples, she offered insightful points. James Charlton is a retired English teacher. He continues to use his admirable instruction skills within the church. His response to my request and the needs of others is a reflection of his faithfulness. I am most grateful to both for help in the completion of this book. Their contributions will be valuable so more people might come into God's kingdom.

To the congregation of Chambersburg First United Methodist Church, who nurtured me in life and encouraged my pioneer efforts in the hospitality ministry, I am extremely grateful. They are a community that continues to grow in God's love, personifying Christ's welcoming acceptance. I hold special gratitude for Rev. Donald Nolder, who, from the beginning of my hospitality ministry, granted me grace, permission, and support and whose personal pastoring in God's hospitality excels.

Charles Salter, my husband, is the best provider and cheerleader ever! Without him, this book would never have happened.

And to God, the Author of all love, who enlightens through the Word and equips through the Spirit, I give endless thanks and praise.

And so I pray: I love you, Lord. May this book serve your purpose and glorify your holy name. Amen.

APPENDIX 1

A Hospitality Gathering
Jazz Event
Here is an example that closely aligns with one church's first attempt
at extending hospitality and teaching hospitality.

3:45–4:10	"Swing Kids": A teenage jazz band plays upbeat music as people gather. Table hosts meet and greet people, especially those for their table.
4:00	Gathering at tables: At each seat there is a place card with a scripture about God's hospitality. Every table has six different scriptures.
4:10	Welcome and greeting: The senior pastor encourages opening up and reaching out to others you do not know.
4:15	Introduction to hospitality: This is given by the hospitality team leader. Then at each table, guests are asked to read aloud the scripture on their place cards and identify who extended hospitality and who received it.
4:25	Three presentations of hospitality by team members: These may be skits, monologues, stories, or speeches. Each is to be five minutes in length.
	Theme 1—Hospitality to Each Other: "Practicing What We Know Is Right"
	Theme 2—Hospitality to Visitors/Guests: "Reaching Out Is Necessary"
	Theme 3—Hospitality to Strangers: "Leaving Our Comfort Zones"
4:45	Table blessing for a light meal with dessert: Throughout the meal, the pastor interjects thoughts on hospitality.
5:05	Evaluating our church's hospitality to visitors: Each person scores and tabulates a questionnaire, rating the church. Table hosts lead discussions about the results. Any eye-opening surprises?
5:30	Table hosts report back to the entire assembly: Sharing the most interesting observations from the church evaluation should prompt more discussion.

5:40	Inspiring music: A solo or spirited communal song is to stir love for others.
5:50	Monologue: Created from the text of Luke 13:10–13, a monologue presents the biblical truth that when touched by Jesus, we are healed to stand tall, see with new eyes, and relate to others.
6:00	Benediction by the pastor while all have joined hands in a friendship circle.

APPENDIX 2

Evaluation of Your Church's Hospitality to Visitors

Yes   No   Give yourself 10 points for each Yes answer, unless otherwise noted, as you
             go through the questions.

——— ———   1. Is there a large sign with inviting words identifying the church? (10 points)

——— ———   2. Does the church have ample parking? (10)

——— ———   3. Is there a specific area in the parking lot designated for visitors? (10)

——— ———   4. Are greeters assigned to the parking lot? (10)

             5. Are there adequate signs
                 outside to the ...

——— ———   a. parking lot? (2)

——— ———   b. church entrances? (2)

                 inside to the ...

——— ———   c. office and restrooms? (2)

——— ———   d. nursery and classrooms? (2)

——— ———   e. sanctuary and other worship locations? (2)

——— ———   6. a. Do all locked outside doors have signs directing where to enter? (5)

——— ———   b. Are all entryways easy to find and convenient to use? (5)

             7. Are there greeters at every entrance ...

——— ———   a. extending a friendly welcome and ready to offer assistance? (5)

——— ———   b. introducing visitors by name to an usher, when appropriate? (5)

             8. Is there a welcome center ...

——— ———   a. with a cordial, helpful attendant? (2)

——— ———   b. that has a directory or layout of the church? (2)

_____ _____   c. providing literature about the church? (2)

_____ _____   d. offering a welcome gift? (2)

_____ _____   e. that is centrally located or easily found with assistance from a satellite location? (2)

                9. Do the ushers …

_____ _____   a. give each newcomer a bulletin and a smile? (2)

_____ _____   b. help a visitor find the nursery or a restroom? (2)

_____ _____   c. offer to help new folks find seats? (2)

_____ _____   d. introduce visitors to other worshippers?(2)

_____ _____   e. ask, "Is there any way I may be of service"? (2)

_____ _____ 10. Do greeters, ushers, and hosts wear name tags so people can easily find help? (10)

_____ _____ 11. Do newcomers have an opportunity to indicate their attendance on a registration pad (name, address, telephone, email, and other information)? (10)

_____ _____ 12. Is the congregation alert to giving a friendly welcome to an outsider? (10)

_____ _____ 13. Does the pastor welcome visitors during the worship service? (Deduct 5 points if visitors are asked to stand, raise their hands, or say their names.) (10)

_____ _____ 14. Do members get the names of newcomers and introduce them to other members? (10)

_____ _____ 15. Are there people in the pews (pew hosts) designated to spot new people, introduce them to other members, and initiate conversation? (10)

_____ _____ 16. Are newcomers invited for coffee or other refreshments, either before or after the service? (10)

_____ _____ 17. Are visitors given an opportunity to meet the pastor? (10)

_____ _____ 18. Are all new folks invited to return? (10)

_____ _____ 19. Is a phone call made, a text sent, a letter written, or a visit made with a small gift to each new person within forty-eight hours? (10)

_____ _____ 20. Is the newcomer encouraged to attend Sunday school, join a small group, get involved with a church function, or participate in a mission project? (10)

Bonus Points

_____ _____ 21. Do members invite others to come and see what God is doing in the lives of people at our church? (10)

_____ _____ 22. Are members who reach out to people in friendship also equipped to share faith, which may help the friend become a believer? (10)

Key for Tabulation

Total your points and see where you fall in the hospitality scale:

0–24	Hostile toward outsiders
25–49	Tolerant (cool) toward visitors
50–74	Visiting is accepted, but not encouraged.
75–99	Lukewarm toward new folks
100–124	Casual preparation for newcomers
125–149	Visiting is encouraged.
150–174	Prepared to make strangers feel important
175–199	Visitors are treated as honored guests and potential members
200–220	Newcomers will know you want them to be part of your fellowship

Author unknown. Adapted by Dianne B. Salter.

APPENDIX 3

Hospitality Tips

[From First United Methodist Church, Chambersburg, PA; used as an educational tool in their church bulletin, one each week for sixteen weeks.]

1. "Contribute to the needs of the saints; practice hospitality." (Romans 12:13 RSV)
2. "So warmly welcome each other into the church, just as Christ has warmly welcomed you; then God will be glorified." (Romans 15:7 TLB)
3. "Those who welcome you are welcoming me. And when they welcome me, they are welcoming God who sent me." (Matthew 10:40 TLB)
4. "Whatever you do, do it with kindness and love." (1 Corinthians 16:14 TLB)
5. "For, dear brothers, you have been given freedom: not freedom to do wrong, but freedom to love and serve each other." (Galatians 5:13 TLB)
6. "You shall love your neighbor as yourself." Love does no wrong to a neighbor; therefore love is the fulfilling of the law." (Romans 13:9–10 RSV)
7. "And who is my neighbor?" (Luke 10:29 RSV). One who is in need and one who tends to that need are neighbors to each other.
8. "Don't forget to be kind to strangers, for some who have done this have entertained angels without realizing it." (Hebrews 13:2 TLB)
9. "I was hungry and you gave me food, I was thirsty and you gave me drink, I was a stranger and you welcomed me, I was naked and you clothed me" (Matthew 25:35–36 RSV).
10. "See how very much our heavenly Father loves us, for he allows us to be called his children—think of it—and we really *are*!" (1 John 3:1 TLB)
11. "And so I am giving a new commandment to you now—love each other just as much as I love you. Your strong love for each other will prove to the world that you are my disciples." (John 13:34–35 TLB)
12. "We offer hospitalia; everything that's ours is yours. When you're here, you're family." (Olive Garden restaurant marketing slogan)

13. People need to be needed.[1]
14. Hospitality reaches out to people wherever they are and welcomes them as they are.[2]
15. The essence of hospitality is to be known and welcomed, needed and loved.[3]
16. Within true hospitality, the roles of host and guest, server and receiver, often become switched.[4]

===

Notes [1-4] are taken from Roger Swanson and Shirley F. Clement, *The Faith-Sharing Congregation* (Nashville: Discipleship Resources, 1999).

APPENDIX 4

Understanding Passing the Peace

Gracious Greetings

From the Old Testament, *shalom* is a traditional Hebrew greeting expressing hope of God's peace for a person. Its most divine meaning reaches far beyond a general sense of well-being, calm within the family, or an absence of war. A greeting is most gracious when both giver and receiver understand the good that is intended. This is not always the norm.

During the formal greeting in a worship service, many members and newcomers alike can be uncomfortable if directed to pass the peace to one another. Even if the directive is understood, the full meaning of the message may not be. If so, the words could be delivered with insufficient power and received with less positive impact. The current culture is not impressed with forced traditions and often does not respond well to them. Yet to live as Christians, we are to greet and welcome strangers graciously.

From my research and personal experience, I have developed strong beliefs about what extending grace to a newcomer should look like. To diminish any discomfort of greeter, receiver, and those waiting to join in, the time allotted for the formal worship greeting should be fairly short. This requires folks to stay within their own general area. Greet a perceived newcomer with a smile, a handshake, words of gladness for his or her presence, and a resolve to get to know him or her better after the service. However, there must be a prevailing awareness to not make anyone feel like a "target." It's the recipient who feels the measure of grace given, not the giver.

Invitation to Receive the Peace of God

The supreme greeting and ultimate welcome were in the words Jesus spoke to the disciples following his resurrection: "Peace be with you" (Luke 24:36; John 20:19, 26). These words, repeated much throughout church history, became known as "passing the peace." But to what *peace* was

Jesus referring? It is the tranquility of heart and mind for a Christian who has trust and hope in God through Jesus himself. To Jesus, having peace meant being right with God and blessed with the joy of knowing so.

Jesus helped people find this peace; so should we. First, our congregations must be educated to understand the peace that God offers; the peace that they themselves should have. Second, they must have the conviction and sincerity to want others to understand and have it also.

God taught the Israelites to welcome the stranger; God instructs us as well. Indeed, we are to give strangers special consideration. A warm and welcoming congregation is to be very conscious of those who may not know what "Peace be with you" means. Our sensitivities and practices in public worship should always be attuned to the needs of newcomers, without failing to attend to our immediate church family.

Some Tokens of Peace in Today's Culture

Reaching out and shaking hands with someone can be as simple as saying hello or as profound as saying, "Peace be with you." It depends upon the setting and context of the greeting, the personal relationship, and mostly, the content of our hearts. If our hearts are home to Jesus, extending our hands to another partially identifies us with the one who extended his life to the point of death to make peace with all humanity—in every time, culture, and lifestyle. The apostle Paul cited this concept to the church at Colossae, as recorded in Colossians 1:20–23.

Our churches should be poised to spread the peace that Jesus paid for. We are called to accept diversity while healing division. We are to create unity without expecting uniformity. In our modern culture, there has been a rapid increase in the ways to greet and welcome others. A very popular choice is having the hug complement or replace the handshake. Some folks like hugs; some don't. The kiss is also becoming more in vogue. Even the early church was encouraged to "greet one another with a holy kiss" (Romans 16:16 NIV). Some like kisses; others don't. Showing and sharing friendship, love, and peace are very scriptural. But if personal boundaries are breached, our intended message may be misread. If you aren't *absolutely* sure that a hug or kiss will be received well, you can always ask, or stick with a handshake or gentle touch.

Whenever our churches extend their hands and open their arms, they become peacemakers. Whatever token of peace is employed in a Christian church, it is to signify a child of God welcoming another child of God. And remember our words are as important as our touch!

Passing the Peace of Christ in Settings Other than Worship

Because there is a biblical model for bestowing peace to those with whom we journey together in faith, we should do it. But public worship is not the only place to invoke peace. Consider passing the peace at the beginning or end of leadership meetings, small-group gatherings, or fellowship meals. Teach children and youth to pass the peace, fist to fist or elbow to elbow, or even team-style. The apostle Paul often echoed our Savior, saying, "Grace and peace be with you." We can do likewise, perhaps in different words: "Rest in God's love." "Have joy in the Lord." "The Spirit gives us hope."

The manner in which we present the peace of God to others largely depends upon where we are on our walk with God. One important aspect about being part of a church family is that each of us is *somewhere* on that walk. So regardless of our ages or other distinctions, if we are involved with the church, we will meet family members along the way, including outside of worship services. And on these occasions, we can practice passing the peace to one another.

The closer our relationship with God, the more desire and confidence we will have for sharing peace. As we rely on the Spirit's presence and encouragement, additional ways and words will become available to us. Here is a thought that might also be helpful: when you offer the peace of God to someone, you are saying, "On my best days, I know what being loved by God feels like, and I want you to know that feeling too."

When we reflect on the meaning of Christ's peace and practice passing it with others already connected to him, we become more willing and better equipped to greet and welcome the stranger. Passing the peace must be done in a way that lovingly communicates the peace God intends. We humans can't create such peace; God does. But as peace comes to us from the heart of Christ, we can pass it on with authority to the hearts of others.

For more information on passing the peace, see Paul Ryan's article "Passing the Peace— Help Your Congregation Embrace a Communal Way of Life," found online at https://www.reformedworship.org/article/march-2011/passing-peace.

APPENDIX 5

A Team with a Heart for God's Hospitality

A Hospitality Workshop

The Purpose

Learn to extend hospitality with a God-like heart.

- *Welcome* the stranger, sincerely care for each one, and do small kindnesses.
- *Invite*, bring, and share your faith with others.
- *Help* connect them to the church family.
- *Minister* to the least of these, exhibiting peace and joy, all to the glory of God.

The Goals

Begin to work as a team.

- *Pray* to stir the Spirit within and receive guidance from God.
- *Organize* ministry tasks.
- *Train* specialized ministers: greeters, ushers, and all hosts.
- *Educate* the congregation.
- *Engage* the congregation.

This concentrated workshop is a series of four parts that will take about six hours. It can be presented in two or four sessions. Strongly encourage commitment to the entire series. Throughout the sessions, the group work is designed to help in articulating the means to the goals and in forming a team that is prepared to pursue them—ready to start or expand the hospitality ministry in your church.

The Workshop

1. Creating an Atmosphere of God's Hospitality

    Part A: Building God's Team
    Part B: A Plan to Reflect God's Heart

2. Living What We Learned

    Part A: Hospitality Ministers: Imitators of God
    Part B: Demonstrating the Goodness of God

If you are interested in this tool for educating your team, contact diannebsalter@gmail.com.

APPENDIX 6

Role-Plays and Skits to Develop Hearts for God's Hospitality

Use the following as role-plays in hospitality team meetings or at a retreat. Then create skits to be used as teaching tools for the congregation at special events or worship services.

Role-Play or Skit 1   **Someone Else's Seat**

Lori enters the church, stops, and looks around. Soon, she is welcomed by a trained greeter: "Hi, I'm Sam. Welcome to_____Church."

"Thank you," she says, "I'm Lori."

Sam, being intentional to help the newcomer feel valued, wanted, loved, and at home, asks, "Will you be joining us for worship?"

She quickly replies, "Yes, I just moved to the area, and I am visiting churches."

Sam smiles and says, "May I help you find a seat?"

"Please," Lori answers.

As they walk together, he points out where the nearest restrooms are located, along with the welcome and refreshment areas. He also invites her to ask him any questions she may have about the church, after the service: "I will be around where we met."

Sam takes Lori to sit with people who are warm and inviting to strangers. He introduces them. And before he leaves, Sam affirms, "We are so glad you are here today!"

Lori responds, "Thank you for helping me find a place. I wouldn't want to sit in someone else's seat."

Discuss: In this scene, what intentions of God, practices of Jesus, and fruit of the Spirit are well represented?

Role-Play or Skit 2   **You're Sitting in My Seat**

Delinquent members for a long time, Bob and Sue, who are husband and wife, enter the church. The greeter at the door welcomes them nicely but does not offer to help them find seats. Somewhat familiar with the church, they decide not to sit in their "old" seats. Instead, they sit closer to the door. A few folks nearby smile at them; others just stare. A short time later, Deidra enters, walks immediately to Bob and Sue's chosen pew, and says, "You're sitting in my seat!" Embarrassed and angered, they move to other seats, but they never come back to the church.

Discuss: Other than Bob and Sue, how could *each* of the characters help turn this episode toward a godly conclusion?

Role-Play or Skit 3   **Mixed Messages**

Tisha and her two children recently moved into an apartment near the church. The congregation is trying to be more intentional about reaching out to the neighborhood. Tisha's family and other neighbors are invited to a church-wide event. As these folks come in, members of the trained hospitality team are prepared to reflect God's presence, welcome, and love. They smile graciously, make eye contact, and initiate friendly conversations that include everyone, adults and children alike. Tisha and her family appreciate the pleasant reception; they return the smiles.

However, they have very little church experience. Soon after being seated, they become restless and noisy. *Some* members close by not only avoid the family but exhibit looks of disapproval and whisper critical comments. Suddenly, Tisha's family feels these people do not want them there, and they wonder, *Does God?*

This occasion exposes the difference between a church just having a hospitality team and one having a congregation with a heart for God's hospitality.

Discuss: Mixed messages can be damaging to any recipient, perhaps even more so to newcomers. Everyone everywhere is to embrace Jesus' second commandment to "love your neighbor as you love yourself." This should be especially evident in God's house.

So how can the hospitality team help the congregation join more fully in this mission reflecting God's heart?

APPENDIX 7

A Four-Week, All-Church Experience
Just Imagine
Your Church Overflowing with God's Hospitality

Weekly Study Descriptions

Table of Contents

I.   Worship Materials: scripture concepts with multiple texts, memory verses, challenges and goals, children's sermon, worship visuals, and true hospitality stories
II. Adult Small-Group Lessons: four weeks plus a follow-up lesson to measure our growth in understanding the Lord's precepts about hospitality and in practicing the examples set forth by the early church
III. Youth-Group Lessons: Collin Moyer, author
IV. Children's Lessons: Grades 1–5; Carel Fish and Bette Renshaw, authors
V.   Daily Devotions: permission to copy—available as handouts to everyone

VI. More Handouts: permission to copy—(1) material on God's hospitality and small kindnesses; (2) eleven actions that build; (3) key fob: *"So that the world may believe"* (John 17:21 NIV); (4) business cards

VII. A six-minute DVD, *Just Imagine*, that embodies the spirit of this entire experience

If you feel your church would benefit from a four-week, intensive, all-church experience that is fully represented by the materials to be provided, contact diannebsalter@gmail.com.

APPENDIX 8

Hospitality Audit

Have each member of a task force do a complete hospitality audit of your church. They should personally observe as many of the items below as possible. For the rest, they should ask people who know. Assign a rating from 1 to 5 in front of each item:

1—very poor; 2—poor; 3—adequate; 4—good; 5—very good

After the task force finishes their individual audits, create a composite audit: the rating for each item is to be the *average* of all the ratings for that item.

Can They Find You?

____ Is your church easy to find? Do you need new signs on major roads or streets near the church?

____ Is your church's name easy to read from the road?

____ Is it easy to tell which entrance to use for the church office? For the sanctuary? For Sunday school? For evening programs?

Are All Areas Inviting?

____ Does the exterior of your church look well maintained and attractive?

____ Does the landscaping need attention?

____ Are there several parking spaces close to the building reserved for the handicapped? For visitors?

____ Are the sidewalks, the entrance, and the interior spaces of the church easy to navigate for persons in wheelchairs or with other mobility concerns?

____ Are the restrooms clean? Without rust or mildew? Do you have lotion and tissues available?

_____ Are all rooms in the church clearly marked? Are there clear directional signs to significant rooms?

_____ Do any rooms need to be cleaned? Painted? Do some rooms look too institutional? Do you have old linoleum or tile that should be replaced with carpet?

Considerate Habits

_____ Do you have adequate lighting in hallways, classrooms, and the sanctuary?

_____ Are there stacks of old bulletins, old magazines, or out-of-date church brochures that should be discarded?

_____ Are there current, attractive handouts or brochures that contain information about your church that would be helpful to visitors?

_____ Are the bulletin boards current? (Visitors are more likely than regular members to read the bulletin boards!)

Get Ready for Company

_____ Are the rooms for infants and toddlers both attractive and clean? Do you have older bedding or toys that should be replaced?

_____ Are extra Bibles and copies of curriculum in the classrooms? Are teachers prepared to teach and trained to welcome visitors?

_____ Are the instructions that are printed in bulletins and spoken in worship services clear to visitors? Remember that you could have visitors who have not been to any church before coming to yours.

_____ Are large-print bulletins available? Is hearing amplification available?

_____ Do you have mints handy for persons who experience coughing or a dry throat during the service?

_____ Does the segment for general announcements, joys, and concerns contain _insider_ references that would make a visitor feel excluded? Do members introduce themselves before sharing with strangers?

_____ Do you have a name-tag system that is current and widely utilized?

_____ Do you have greeters positioned at the entrances to the church? Are greeters and ushers prepared to welcome visitors? Do you offer training for greeters and ushers?

_____ Are most members of the congregation ready to welcome visitors? Do you provide hospitality training?

Connecting

___ Are refreshments available at a fellowship time and/or during Sunday school classes?

___ Do you have many members who go out of their way to greet visitors and introduce them to others?

___ Are members of your church inclined to offer brunch or dinner invitations to your guests?

___ Do you have a system in place to respond to visitors within forty-eight hours of their attendance by leaving a small gift at their homes? Freshly baked cookies or bread, a devotional booklet, flowers, or a mug with your church's name are all possibilities.

___ Interview people who have recently visited your church, ask them for feedback, and encourage them to return. Talk to people who have continued to come—and to those who haven't.

Christian Community, Fort Wayne, Indiana

Adapted by Edward Wentz

APPENDIX 9

Views of the Institutional Church

People outside looking in often make adverse generalizations about the church. Their perceptions may or may not be true. But our churches should have positive responses to override—maybe even change—negative opinions. A study by Clapp and Detwiler[1] reflects some of the ideas people hold about the various faith traditions in our current culture.

- *Evangelical congregations* are fast-growing and often viewed as being more interested in a person's spiritual scalps, volunteer hours, and money than in the person as an individual.
- *Fundamentalist and conservative congregations* are often considered as hotbeds of right-wing politics. The unchurched feel that these churches do not really want you unless you share their political views.
- *Mainline Protestant congregations* are considered more open to diversity of belief and lifestyle but are also seen as stodgy and not very open to change. They are also perceived as not necessarily able or willing to help with spiritual issues.
- *Anabaptist congregations* are not well known by those outside their traditions. Mennonite and Brethren churches are viewed by the unchurched as closed circles, with the assumption being you are basically born into the denomination. They are also viewed as having a strong peace and justice heritage.
- *Roman Catholic congregations* are better known by the unchurched but not necessarily better understood. Many misconceptions exist around the role of the pope, the conduct of the priests, and several aspects of parish life. The unchurched often see positions on birth control and women in the priesthood as barriers.

Steve Clapp and Sam Detwiler, *Sharing Living Water: Evangelism as Caring Friendship* (Christian Community Resources, 2001), 23–24.

ENDNOTES

Chapter 1: Living a Life of Love

1   Tom Wright, *Paul for Everyone: Romans Part Two, Chapters 9–16* (Louisville: Westminster John Knox Press, 2004), 113.
2   John Koenig, *New Testament Hospitality: Partnership with Strangers as Promise and Mission* (Philadelphia: Fortress Press, 1985), ix.
3   Ibid., x.
4   Ibid., 29.

Chapter 3: God's Royal Decree

1   Cheryl Somers-Ingersol, *Disciplines: A Book of Daily Devotions 2013* (Nashville: Upper Room, 2013), 137.
2   John Koenig, *New Testament Hospitality: Partnership with Strangers as Promise and Mission* (Philadelphia: Fortress Press, 1985), 31.
3   Herbert Lockyer, ed., *Nelson's Illustrated Bible Dictionary* (Nashville: Thomas Nelson Publishers, 1986), 937.
4   Koenig, *New Testament Hospitality*, 8.
5   Henry Nouwen, *Reaching Out: The Three Movements of the Spiritual Life* (New York: Image/ Doubleday, 1975), 45.
6   Susquehanna Conference of the United Methodist Church (SUSUMC), Elder's Day Apart, April 10, 2013.
7   Michael Collopy and Mother Teresa, *Works of Love Are Works of Peace: Mother Teresa of Calcutta and the Missionaries of Charity: A Photographic Record* (San Francisco: Ignatius, 1996), 49.
8   E. Stanley Jones, *Mastery: The Art of Mastering Life* (London: Hodder & Sloughton, 1946), 18.
9   Norman Shawchuck, Philip Kotler, et. al., *Marketing for Congregations: Choosing to Serve People More Effectively* (Nashville: Abingdon Press, 1992), 76.
10 Dan R. Dick, "Offering Christ in a Culture of Fear," *Circuit Rider Magazine*, Nov/Dec/Jan 2008–09 (Nashville: Ministry Matters), 24–25.
11 Steve Clapp and Fred Bernhard, *Hospitality: Life in a Time of Fear, Finding Meaning and Purpose in a Fearful World* (Life Quest, 2002), 177.
12 John Thompson and Randy Scruggs, "Sanctuary," *The Faith We Sing* (Nashville: Abingdon Press, 2000), 2164.
13 Will L. Thompson, "Softly and Tenderly Jesus Is Calling," Music and Text by Will Lamartine Thompson (Chicago: Thompson Music Company, 1880).

Chapter 4: Learning and Teaching the Heart of God

1   Bill Dockery, "Wisdom Without Words," *Disciplines, A Book of Daily Devotions 2015* (Nashville: Upper Room, 2015), 74.

2   "True Stories of Random Acts," *Reader's Digest* (New York: Reader's Digest, October 2015), 90.

3   Blaise Pascal and W. F. Trotter, *Pascal's Pensees* (London: J. M. Dent & Sons, 1931), 278.

4   *The Interpreter's Bible Commentary, Vol. 1, Genesis, Exodus, Leviticus* (Nashville: Abingdon Press, 1996), 946.

5   Herbert Lockyer, ed., *Nelson's Illustrated Bible Dictionary* (Nashville: Thomas Nelson Publishers, 1986), 697, 444, 1108, 1010, 392.

6   John Koenig, *New Testament Hospitality: Partnership with Strangers as Promise and Mission* (Philadelphia: Fortress Press, 1985), 16; cf., S. H. Dresner, *The Sabbath* (New York: Burning Bush Press, 1970), 54.

7   Luke 7:36–50.

8   Koenig, *New Testament Hospitality*, 17; cf., E.L. Sukenik, *Ancient Synagogues in Palestine and Greece* (London: British Academy/Oxford, 1934), 49, 69–70.

9   Matt. 21:12–17; Mark 11:15–19; Luke 19:45–48; John 2:13–25.

10 Ralph Carmichael, "I Looked for Love," *I Looked for Love* (Nashville: Lexicon Music, 1969), 38.

11 Marjorie Thompson, *Soul Feast: An Invitation to the Christian Spiritual Life* (Louisville: Westminster John Knox Press, 1995), 123; cf., Matthew Fox, iconoclastic Dominican scholar turned Episcopal priest, originator of "Creation Spirituality" Original Blessings (Santa Fe, NM: Bear Company, 1983), 112–13.

12 Parker J. Palmer, *The Company of Strangers: Christians and the Renewal of America's Public Life* (New York: Crossroad, 1983), 26.

13 Francis Collins, as told to Tim Hench, "His Beautiful World," *Guideposts*, vol. LXI, 10 (Danbury, CT: Guideposts, December 2006), 42–44.

14 Pamela Rose Williams, "18 Powerful Francis A. Schaeffer Quotes," *What Christians Want to Know*: http://www.whatchristianswanttoknow.com/18-powerful-francis-a-schaeffer-quotes/#ixzz4Wo0Oq7Hw (March 25, 2019).

Chapter 5: Practicing Active Love

1   Red Carpet Hospitality Seminar, Chris Walker, leader; Central Presbyterian Church, Chambersburg, PA, September 26, 2015.

2   "Top 25 Quotes by Francis Schaeffer," *AZ Quotes*: http://www.azquotes.com/author/13063-Francis_Schaeffer (March 25, 2019).

3   Carl Arico, Mary Anne Best, and others, contributors, *The Contemplative Life Program: 40-day Practice: Hospitality* (Wilkes-Barre, PA: Contemplative Outreach, Ltd., 2007), 46.

4   Steve Sjogren and Dave Ping, *Out Flow: Outward-Focused Living in a Self-Focused World* (Loveland, TX: Group Publishing, 2006), 195.

5   Illustration courtesy of Edward Wentz.

6   Acts 2:43–47.

7   Marjorie J. Thompson, *Soul Feast: An Invitation to the Christian Spiritual Life* (Louisville: Westminster John Knox Press, 1995), 134.

8   Red Carpet Hospitality Seminar.

9   Matthew 11:19.

10   Luke 4:18.

11   John 15:15.

12   Luke 23; John 19.

13   Matthew 16:19; described in book of Acts.

14   Red Carpet Hospitality Seminar.

15   Francis Thompson (1859–1907), "The Hound of Heaven," poem found in *The Oxford Book of English Mystical Verse*, Nicholson & Lee, eds., 1917.

16   John O. Gooch, *Being a Christian in the Wesley Tradition: Belonging/Believing/Living/ Growing* (Nashville: Discipleship Resources, 2009), 55.

17   Ibid. 55–56.

18   Hillsong, "At the Cross," Zscheeck and Morgan, composers; *YouTube Highpraise.com*, Up loaded January 20, 2008: https://www.youtube.com/watch?v=eOY0mjjmx8Y (March 25, 2019).

19   John 15:6–8.

20   Thom and Joani Schultz, "Why Nobody Wants to Go to Church Any More," workshop.

21   Thom S. Rainer, "Hope for Dying Churches": https://factsandtrends.net/2018/01/16/hope-for-dying-churches (March 25, 2019).

22   "Quotes by Oscar Wilde," *Goodreads*: https://www.goodreads.com/quotes/search?utf8=%E2%9C%93&q=every+saint+has+a+past&commit=Search (March 25, 2019).

23   Peter Scholtes, words and music, "They'll Know We Are Christians," *The Faith We Sing* (Nashville: Abingdon Press, 2000), 2243.

Chapter 6: What's a Church to Do?

1   Robert Schnase, "The Practice of Radical Hospitality," *Five Practices of Fruitful Congregations* (Nashville: Abingdon Press, 2007), 11.

2   Ibid.

3   Jeffrey D. Wilson, "The Baker's Dozen of Church Growth," *Workshop on Biblical Hospitality and the Vital Church* (Oakland Church of the Brethren Teaching Congregation; Fred Bernhard, leader), 42.

4   Albert L. Winseman, "Growing an Engaged Church," information included in a pastor's packet, Central Pennsylvania Conference United Methodist Church, currently SUSUMC.

5   Marjorie J. Thompson, "Entertaining Angels Unawares, The Spirit of Hospitality," *Soul Feast* (Louisville: Westminster John Knox Press, 1995), 126.

6   Christine D. Pohl, "Ancient and Biblical Sources," *Making Room: Recovering Hospitality as a Christian Tradition* (Grand Rapids, MI: Eerdmans, 1999), 34.

7   Adam Hamilton, "The Fourth Question," *Leading Beyond the Walls: Developing Congregations with a Heart for the Unchurched* (Nashville: Abingdon Press, 2002), 29.

8   Fred Kaan, "Help Us Accept Each Other," *The United Methodist Hymnal, Book of United Methodist Worship* (Nashville: The United Methodist Publishing House, 1989), 560.

9   Corpus Christi Catholic Church, Chambersburg, PA, 2013. A creed composed by this congregation, used in mass.

10   Scott Bowerman, "A Church That Welcomes," sermon posted on Facebook, Central Presbyterian Church, Chambersburg, PA, October 2013.

Chapter 7: Let a Team Begin

1   Nelson Searsy, *Fusion: Turning First-Time Guests into Fully-Engaged Members of Your Church* (Grand Rapids, MI: Baker Book House, 2002), 62.

2   Roger K. Swanson, Shirley F. Clement, *The Faith-Sharing Congregation: Developing a Strategy for the Congregation as Evangelist* (Nashville: Discipleship Resources, 1996).

3   First United Methodist Church, Chambersburg, PA, 2002.

4   Carl Arico, Mary Anne Best, and others, contributors, *The Contemplative Life Program: 40- day Practice: Hospitality* (Wilkes-Barre, PA: Contemplative Outreach, Ltd., 2007), 46.

5   Alfred, Lord Tennyson, "Idylls of the King" (CreateSpace Independent Publishing Platform, September 28, 2017).

6   Oswald Chambers, "Spontaneous Love, April 30," *My Utmost for His Highest* (Grand Rapids, MI: Oswald Chambers Publications Assn., Ltd., 1935), 121.

7   Red Carpet Hospitality Seminar, Chris Walker, leader; Central Presbyterian Church, Chambersburg, PA, September 26, 2015.

Chapter 8: Expectations of Hospitality Ministers

1   Jim Forest, "Opening Heart and Home," *Sojourners Magazine*, vol. 33, No. 7, July 2004, n.p.

2   John Henry Cardinal Newman (1801-1890), "Radiating Christ," *Spirituality for Today*, vol. 5, iss. 3, October, 1999: http://spirituality.org/is/051/home.asp (March 25, 2019).

Chapter 9: God's Invitation Is to All

1   Andy Stanley, *Go Fish* (Portland, OR: Multnomah, 2005), 36.

2   Adam Hamilton, "The Fourth Question," *Leading Beyond the Walls: Developing Congregations with a Heart for the Unchurched* (Nashville: Abingdon Press, 2002), 29.

Chapter 10: Sharing Our Faith

1   Rom. 10:14 CEV.

2   Andy Stanley, *Go Fish* (Portland, OR: Multnomah, 2005), 9–10.

3   Ahka, compiler, "Gandhi's advice to Christians through Dr. E. Stanley Jones," online video clip. *YouTube*, August 6, 2009: http://youtu.be/bQHIjCLcF6o (March 25, 2019).

4   Ibid.

5   John Fischer, "Flunking Witnessing," *The Purpose Driven Life Daily Devotional*, September 22, 2006 (Lake Forest, CA: Purpose Driven Ministries, 2006).

6   Ibid.

7   Steve Sjogren and Dave Ping, *Out Flow: Outward-Focused Living in a Self-Focused World* (Loveland, TX: Group Publishing, 2006), 71.

8   Becky Benenate and Joseph Durepos, eds., "On Prayer," *Mother Teresa, No Greater Love* (Novato, CA: New World Library, 1997), 5.

9   Ibid, 3–6.

10 Hebrews 13:5.

11 Ephesians 3:19–20.

12 Clapp and Detwiler, "In Over Our Heads," *Sharing Living Water: Evangelism as Caring Friendship* (Elgin, IL: Brethren Press, 2000), 102.

13 Henry Nouwen, *Reaching Out: The Three Movements of the Spiritual Life* (New York: Image/ Doubleday, 1975), 45.

14 N. T. Wright, *Simply Christian: Why Christianity Makes Sense* (San Francisco: HarperOne, 2006), 56.

15 Talbot W. Chambers, *The New York City Noon Prayer Meeting: A Simple Prayer Gathering That Changed the World* (Wagner Publications, 2002).

16 Matthew 13:31.

17 1 Corinthians 3:6.

18 Clapp and Detweiler, Ibid., 99.

19 Gene Edwards, ed., *Practicing His Presence: Brother Lawrence and Frank Laubach* (Jacksonville, FL: The Seed Sowers, 1973), 36.

Chapter 11: The Least and the Lost Are Loved by God

1   Robert Lupton, *Theirs Is the Kingdom: Celebrating the Gospel in Urban America* (New York: Harper One, 1981), 99.

2   Rudy Rasmus, "He Touched Them," *Touch: The Power of Touch in Transforming Lives* (Friendswood, TX: Baxter Press and Spirit Rising Music, 2006), 60.

3   Lupton, 98.

4   Parker J. Palmer, *The Company of Strangers: Christians and the Renewal of America's Public Life* (New York: Crossroad, 1983).

5   John Koenig, *New Testament Hospitality: Partnership with Strangers as Promise and Mission* (Philadelphia: Fortress Press, 1985), ix.

6   *Mother Teresa*, edited and introduced by Fr. Brian Kolodiejehuk, M.C., "Mother Teresa's Call," *Jesus Is My All in All: Praying with the "Saints of Calcutta"* (New York: Doubleday, 2008), 1–3.

7   Michael Collopy and Mother Teresa, *Works of Love Are Works of Peace: Mother Teresa of Calcutta and the Missionaries of Charity: A Photographic Record* (San Francisco: Ignatius, 1996), 28.

8   Ibid., *Introduction*.

9   Jose Luis Gonzalez-Balado, compiler, *Mother Teresa: In My Own Words, 1910-1997* (New York: Gramercy Books, 1996), 24.

10 Rasmus, 148.

11 Alan Menken and Stephen Schwartz, "God Helps the Outcasts" (EMI Mills Music, Inc./ Greydog Music, 1996).

12 Rasmus, 17, 25, 19, 45, 51, 79, 86, 124.
13 Ibid., 207.
14 Palmer, 65.
15 Lupton, 112.
16 George R. Plagenz, "Some Churches Need More Warmth" (Greenfield, IN: *The Daily Reporter*, March 18, 2006), 7.
17 Daniel L. Schutte, "Here I Am, Lord" (Carol Stream, IL: Hope Publishing), text and music, 1981.

AUTHOR BIOGRAPHY

PHOTOGRAPHER: COLLEEN GOUGE

Dianne Salter lives with her husband, Chuck, in a beautiful rural valley surrounded by urban development in South Central Pennsylvania. Care and upkeep of their home and mountain cabin are duties of devotion that create welcoming space for family, friends, and even strangers.

Believing all humans are created to be in relationship with God and others, she pursues such loving community. In intimate times alone, where God's love comes to her most fully in Christ Jesus, her soul is restored so she might channel his love in relationships with others.

Three amazing adult children and their spouses, eight grandchildren, two foreign students and their families, and a youth from her church who needed a home after graduation bless her life. All are considered family and call her Mom or Gran.

Education in college and seminaries, throughout much of Dianne's adult life, earned degrees, certifications, and ordination for professions as public school educator, director of Christian

Education, and Minister of Evangelism. She was privileged to work with nursery school children through adults, in classrooms and pulpits, from the security of the church setting to vulnerable places in the community. Extended family, lifelong friends, new neighbors, and friends in low places enrich her life. Children, youth, those outside the church, and the least of these deserve special attention.

Challenging and rewarding is how she describes her ministry to welcome people into God's kingdom. Inviting Christians to become partners with God, as a host to all who have not yet come to adopt the fullness of God's love for themselves, is a lifestyle change. It is not easily done, as it involves surrender and trust. Her passion continues to bring into God's house the 80 percent of people in the United States who have no meaningful relationship with a church. In this coming-home atmosphere, decisions for following Jesus, loving God with all our hearts, and loving our neighbors as ourselves can bring about the community God longs to exist. And that happens one person at a time.

She invites us to just imagine what might happen if every person who comes into our space is treated as a special guest; none treated as strangers. Every time one child of God comes home, joy overflows! For that reason, she continues as speaker, consultant and seminar leader for God's Hospitality.

Connect with Dianne at justimaginegodshospitality.com. To those of you who have read this book, if you have plans to be in South Central Pennsylvania, contact Dianne at diannebsalter@gmail.com. She invites you to her home. She would love to meet you.

"In light of all this, here's what I want you to do … get out there and
walk—better yet, run!—on the road God called you to travel."
(Ephesians 4:1 The Message)

Printed in the United States
By Bookmasters